HOW TO BUILD A BIKE

HOW TO BUILD A BIKE

A SIMPLE GUIDE TO MAKING YOUR OWN RIDE

JENNI GWIAZDOWSKI

FRANCES
LINCOLN

Hi there. I'm your host, Jenni Gwiazdowski. I probably don't look like a mechanic. I probably don't look like your average bike buff: I'm not grumpy nor covered in grease (not all the time, at least). But since March 2012 I have helped thousands of people fix their own bikes, as well as plan and build their dream bikes, at London Bike Kitchen. LBK is a DIY open workshop: we teach people maintenance skills, and provide a welcoming space for people to learn about and work on their bicycles. 'Build Your Own Bike' is one of our most popular classes at LBK. It's actually the reason why I set up the workshop in the first place - I wanted to take a class where I could learn how to put a bike together, but it didn't exist. Over the years, I've been pleasantly surprised by how many other people feel the same way.

WHY BUILD A BIKE?

Why build a bike? The question you should be asking yourself is: why not? Bikes are rad. They're amazing machines that cure so many of society's ills - they save money, cut pollution, facilitate exercise, nurture mental health. And they're also radically democratic. Anyone can own a bike, and what's more, just about anyone can build one too. Studies have shown that working with your hands is incredibly fulfilling, confidence building, empowering even. Plus, it's the mode of transport for the impending zombie apocalypse. Two birds!

'ME? CAN I BUILD A BIKE?'

Perhaps you're on the fence. Maybe you think building a bike is something you can't physically do. Or won't have time for. Well, I'm here to tell you that it's definitely within your powers. I wasn't always handy with a spanner – I used to have soft, poet's hands. I worked in marketing! I dabbled with tools, I knitted and crocheted – but it wasn't until this reckless desire to build my own bike emerged that I gravitated towards the DIY side. It turned out to be one of the most satisfying things I've ever done. Look at it this way, if you don't give it a go, you've already built nothing.

You've also got a wealth of knowledge at your fingertips (and I'm not just talking about this book). The internet is a blessing and a curse, full of information, sometimes conflicting and confusing. I recommend starting with Sheldon Brown. Sheldon is sadly not with us anymore, but he was a workshop mechanic in Massachusetts. He was also the ultimate bike geek and the absolute boss when it came to knowledge of bicycle systems. His web 1.0 site is fantastic to dive into if you need more information.

ANYONE CAN GET HANDY WITH TOOLS. ANYONE.

This book is for everybody who loves cycling and wants to get more involved in how their bike works, learn new skills and generally get stuck in. Gender has nothing to do with nuts, bolts or tools; some of the best mechanics I know are women.

I want this book to be a stepping stone into the bike world for those who are not generally encouraged to pick up tools. The difference I see in people before and after they work on their bikes for the first time is striking. LBK teaches people from all backgrounds, and the most common remark is: 'I didn't think I'd be able to do that,' along with a smile.

Before you begin…
Building your own bike is extremely rewarding, and will provide you with a wonderful machine that will give you useful service for years. It is a challenge – that's why it's fun! But don't expect a bicycle straight away. This is a project that could potentially take weeks, or even months. However, remember: nothing worth it was ever easy. This is going to be a labour of love, and if you commit to that, you'll be pleased with the results.

WHY BUILD A SINGLE-SPEED BIKE?

Gears on a bike exist for a reason: they make the rider more efficient, and uphill travel becomes a breeze. But lots of us live in busy cities, where we have to stop and start (and stop and start, and stop and start) on our daily rides. Changing gears becomes a chore. We stop doing it. And that makes the parts wear down faster – that one single sprocket that you keep riding in becomes worn and you have to replace the whole cassette.

Plus, unless you commute to work in the mountains, chances are you don't go up and down huge hills every day. But if there are a few, choose an easy gearing (explained in more detail on p94) to give your knees a break as you build up those quads.

So this is the case for the single-speed bike. It has fewer components, so the bike is lighter, and the components that *are* there are more robust, lasting longer than those on a geared bike. It's cleaner, simpler, sleeker. Less to go wrong. And it can still take a pannier rack to hold your stuff. It's easier for a beginner to build, too.

WHAT WILL YOUR BICYCLE END UP LOOKING LIKE?

Assumptions are the mother of all fuck-ups, this is true. But since I don't know you, dear reader, I am forced to make some. We need to get a bit technical here, but don't let that scare you away. Even if you don't know what all this means right now, you will soon. Study the big bicycle diagram inside the cover flaps too.

Let's establish something: the bike you're intending to build is a simple single-speed with front and rear rim brakes. A steel frame is preferred. Why? I often hear people say they think steel is heavy, or old-fashioned. Think again – steel is real. The advantages are many: steel frames are more comfortable to ride; they're more durable and can take scratches and minor dents; they have more painting options; and actually, steel is stronger than aluminium.

We're going to be working mainly with a classic 'diamond' frame, the sort you have to swing your leg over to get on. It has been the dominant shape for over 100 years for a reason – it's strong and it flexes out far less than other shapes, making it more efficient for the pedaller. But you can use other shapes too: the step-through, like you see everyone riding in Amsterdam, is good if you want to keep your yourself more upright. The mixte is an ideal in-between: this is a step-through frame with a split top tube, which gives the arrangement extra rigidity. I'd recommend trying to get one of these if you want a step-through. Putting one of these together is more or less the same procedure for the diamond frame as described in this book.

There are a few more technical requirements that we'll go over in more detail later on (in the chapter Choosing Your Frame). But know that a single-speed is a great place to start learning about how to put a bike together, and once you master this, you can move on to geared bikes, disc brakes, recumbents or any other hot wheeled machine that tickles your fancy. It will also make you more confident with basic maintenance, and less-competent pals might ask you to change their inner tube or chain in exchange for beer. Sounds like a good trade to me.

Also, you know how to use basic tools. I'm talking about hex keys, screwdrivers and spanners. Righty tighty, lefty loosey, that sort of thing.

But – you're not a bike mechanic. This book is for enthusiastic beginners, and I won't be going into the nitty-gritty details about the difference in electronic shifting versus hub gears, or 1980s Specialized Rockhoppers vs 1990s Specialized Rockhoppers. (That's what the internet is for.)

And finally, you will have to spend a little money when the time calls for it. Building a bike isn't necessarily a cheap exercise – it can be, but you will need to invest in some decent consumables to create a safe bicycle. Good tyres, brake pads, chain, cables – these parts are designed to wear down, and putting on secondhand versions could mean compromising your safety and the safety of others. Who wants that? But a bit of investment at this stage will mean you end up with a bicycle which, with a bit of minor maintenance, will keep you moving for the forseeable future.

So what will your bicycle end up looking like? Shiny, smart, cool, unique, safe, new and totally yours.

VELO VOCABULARY

The world of the bicycle can sound bewilderingly complicated to those who have never dipped their toe in. Just as the world of brewing, or bee-keeping, or biology can, to newcomers. However, all you need to know is a few simple terms and you'll feel much better about the task ahead. You're not aiming to become a professional mechanic, just to clarify some basic definitions that will keep us all speaking the same language.

Age
Modern = 1990s and onward; vintage = 1980s and earlier.

Alloy
A mixture of two elements, one of which is a metal. In the bike world, 'alloy' is taken to mean aluminium alloy, used for some frames, wheels and components; steel is also an alloy (of iron and carbon, mainly), but we just call it steel.

Bearing system
A collection of components consisting of ball bearings, cup and cone, allowing for rotation. Sealed bearings exist in an enclosed system. Types include bottom bracket (BB), headset, hub, pedals.

Drive-side
When on your bike, the right side of your bike, where the chain is.

Flush
When one component lies perfectly flat against another; it's neither recessed nor protruding. For example, brake pads need to be flush with the rim in order for them to work properly - the whole pad should be parallel in all axes to the braking surface.

Frameset
The combination of frame and forks.

Freewheel
A ratcheted sprocket screwed on to a rear wheel which allows pedalling and coasting (travelling without pedalling, ie down a hill).

Headset
The bearings system that attaches the fork to the frame and allows it to turn (see p97).

Hex key/Allen key
A six-sided tool. The brand name Allen key is famous, but we will be using the term hex key.

Leverage
Mechanical advantage or power gained by using a lever. For bike building, we mean a long-handled rigid bar that pivots at one point used to move an object at a second point by a force applied at a third point. You can add leverage by extending the lever handle of the tool you're working with (like with a big hollow tube). Think see-saw.

Loosen
To turn anticlockwise, generally speaking. There are, though,
a couple of points on the bike where turning clockwise will loosen a bolt or nut. See also: Tighten.

Non-drive-side
When on your bike, the left side of your bike.

Play
If something is loose that shouldn't be, it has play. On a bicycle it generally happens when there's a bearing system that's not tight enough. The general way to check for play is to move whatever is meant to spin in the direction that it shouldn't spin. So if, for example, a pedal is meant to spin around and around: test for play by moving the pedal up and down, in the direction perpendicular to its desired movement.

Purchase
When a tool has full contact and grip with the part it is going to move.

Rounding
When the straight angles of a bolt's head are rounded off (see the picture, above right). This can happen with both hex and socket bolts if you use the wrong-sized tool or don't have purchase when using the tool. To avoid, make sure

that tool is fully fitted, and not at an angle, before applying force. For example, a hex key should be fully pushed inside the bolt socket before turning it.

Stripping

When threads on a bolt, for example, become flattened (see above left). Usually caused by screwing in the bolt crooked, poor quality components, mismatched thread pitch, and/or over-tightening. To avoid stripped threads, tighten first by hand. If it stops after a couple of turns and the threads are fairly clean, you may have mismatched thread pitch and will need to find a replacement.

Thread

Helical ridges or grooves cut into a bolt or screw. Thread pitch is the distance between the threads on a bolt or screw. These can vary depending on the size of the part, and where the part is from, among other things. The important thing to remember is that thread pitches can differ and, if you have trouble screwing in something, you may need to change the component for one with a pitch that matches.

Tighten

To turn clockwise, generally speaking. There are, though, a couple of points on the bike where turning anticlockwise will tighten a bolt/nut. Comes in different degrees: to finger tighten is to only use your fingers to screw something in. Hand tightening is to apply a bit more force with your whole hand. And to shoulder tighten is to engage your entire arm and shoulder to tighten something using the appropriate tool. Many components should first be finger tightened to make sure they are going in correctly, and then a tool can be used to get the correct torque.

The size of the tool used dictates how tight something should be. You can't apply a huge amount of force with a 2.5mm hex key, so don't try. Small tool = tight but not mega-Hulk-tight.

There are three points on the bike that have a reverse thread: the drive-side cup on British thread bottom brackets, the lockring on a fixed wheel sprocket, and the non-drive-side pedal. If you're tightening something and it's not catching at all, it may be because you have to turn the other way.

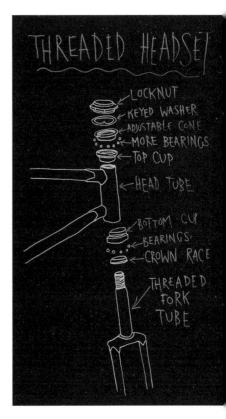

Washers

Flat circular metal rings that help spread the load of a bolt. They are usually used next to a nut.

TOOLS & EQUIPMENT

Back in the day, bikes only needed three tools - a hammer, a spanner and a screwdriver. Boy, have times changed. Bikes now require more and more specialist tools, some quite expensive. If you have a local community bike space, now's your chance to get acquainted with it. Or pool your funds with a group of friends for a tool share. This chapter's an overview of all the tools you may need for your build. Don't purchase any just yet, but see which ones you already have, and get familiar with the ones you don't.

NEED TO HAVE

Crown race setter

Chainbreaker

14mm socket

Adjustable spanner

Headset press

1" headcup remover

Crank puller

Pliers

Cable cutters

Hammer

Punch

Tyre
levers

Hex keys

Combination
spanner set

BIKE-BUILDING MANTRAS
TO HELP YOU AT EVERY TURN

* Righty tighty, lefty loosey

* Metal on metal (using a
  hammer on a metal tool or
  part will provide the best
  power transfer)

* You are stronger pushing
  down than pulling up

* Use a longer lever if things
  get stuck

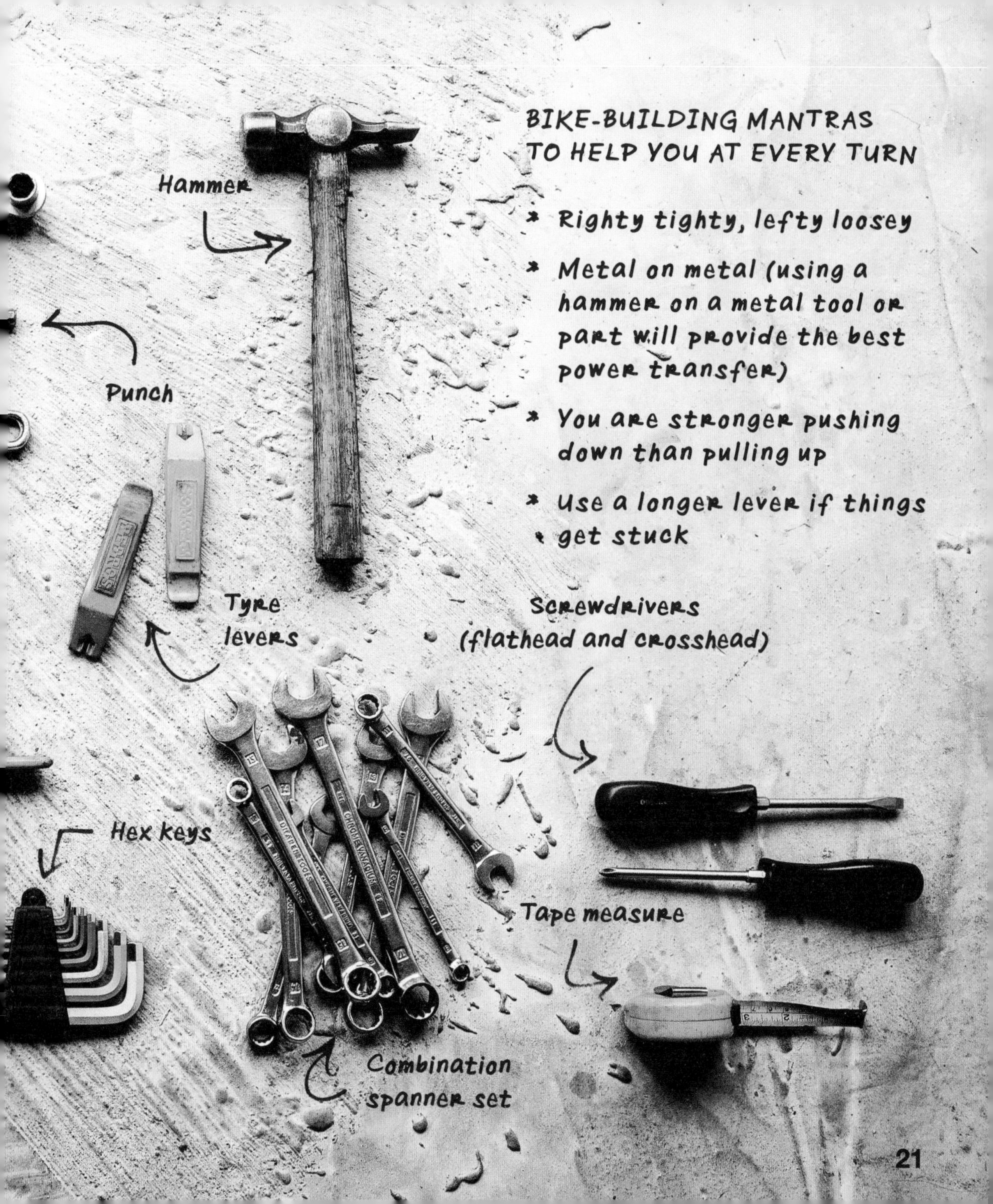

Screwdrivers
(flathead and crosshead)

Tape measure

NICE TO HAVE

Freewheel removers

Single-speed chain whip and lockring tool

PlusGas - for seized parts

PlusGas
FORMULA A

FAST RELEASE
DISMANTLING LUBRICANT

LUBRICATES, CLEANS, PROTECTS AND DISPLACES MOISTURE

500 ml

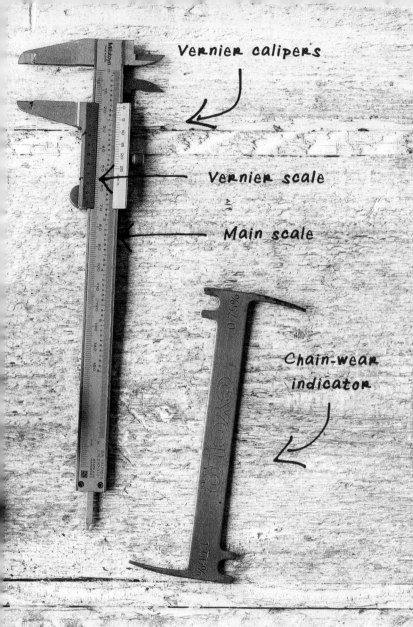

Vernier calipers

Vernier scale

Main scale

Chain-wear indicator

How to use vernier calipers
This is one of the most useful measuring tools. It can precisely measure the inside diameter, outside diameter and depth of an object, up to two decimal places. Start by using the correct function for the measurement you require: inside diameter, outside diameter or depth. Press the caliper arms against the object then gently tighten the screw clamp to hold this measurement in place. The first reading is on the main scale. The '0' mark will determine your first number reading. The second reading is on the vernier scale. Locate where the first numbered tick mark on the vernier scale lines up with a tick mark on the main scale. Add the first number to the second to get the total measurement. It's simpler than it sounds, honest!

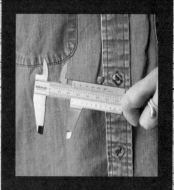

And a workstand will make things easier!

LUBRICATING MATERIALS

Grease - lithium grease is cheap, but there are nicer versions. Try Weldtite or Motorex

Oil - to be used on exposed parts, like chains. Use a biodegradable one like Pedro's Chainj

Cleaning materials, like bike-specific cleaner and chain degreaser

Anti-seize - aka copper paste. Its tiny copper flakes will prevent threads from seizing up

The difference between oil and grease

Oil goes on parts on the outside of your bike, and grease goes in places that don't see the light of day. This is because of a difference in viscosity. Grease is thick, and is great at reducing friction of bearings – but it can attract loads of dirt and grit, which is why it's put inside your bike. Oil is less viscous and only goes on moving parts which are exposed to the elements. While oil doesn't attract as much dirt as grease would, because it's on the outside of your bike, it will attract some anyway, so it's important to clean these parts regularly. Plus: never get oil on rims, brake pads or tyres!

Grease

Oil

Homemade tools

I literally have a workshop full of professional tools at my greasy fingertips, which is why I've used a few of them in this book. However, that's not to say you wouldn't be able to totally DIY your way through this. There are loads of tutorials online for making your own bike tools, and methods involving the basics like a hammer, screwdriver and adjustable spanner. That said, I do recommend seeking out your local community bike space, where you can learn how to use more technical tools. The right tool for the right job will work wonders, and I bet they'd love to have you over too. And if you don't have one nearby, well maybe you should just start one up…

Imperial vs metric

A long time ago in a galaxy far, far away, some English king decided on some arbitrary measurements and behold: imperial sizing was born. Bikes are covered in a confusing array of metric and imperial measurements. Headsets are 1", bottom brackets are 68mm, and tyres are 700 x 25 (700 actually means nothing but the 25 *does* mean 25mm). Where imperial vs metric comes into play, though, is when you need the correctly sized tool for the job – modern bikes will pretty much only require metric tools. But older bikes may need some imperial spanners. If you use a metric spanner on a nut or bolt, and find that it seems to be in between sizes, chances are it's imperial. If you can, get the corresponding spanner, but if you can't, use an adjustable spanner and be very careful not to slip. It would be great if you could switch the component with a metric replacement, but different thread pitches may make this impossible. Also, this does not mean that metric is the system of measurement for The Rebellion. (Star Wars? No? I'll leave it.)

Cleaning your hands

• If you don't want to wear gloves, I recommend this fantastic DIY hand scrub, gentler and more environmentally friendly than Swarfega. Use old coffee grounds mixed with washing-up liquid (dishwashing detergent), or if you can bear to part with it, a nice hand soap. The grounds will scrub off any grime and the soap will cut through the grease. If you want to experiment, add coconut oil. Make it in small batches as it can go off if you don't use it often. Keep unused portions in the fridge. But any which way you use it, you will end up with sparkling, soft hands, guaranteed.

• If you get any oil or grease on your clothes, don't despair. The Buncha Farmers All Natural Stain Stick works wonders!

CHOOSING YOUR FRAME

The frame is the heart and soul of a bike. When people say they like your bike, they probably mean they like your frame. (Unless they're secret handlebar fetishists. There are some.) And different people will like different aspects of frames - some superficial, some structural. You could start with colour (like I did, when I chose my very first road bike), but I would suggest starting with a short lesson in frame geometry, and then A QUIZ. It is very important you read this whole chapter before diving into making your own bike - you want the right kind of bike for you!

GEOMETRY

Frame geometry is a big factor in your riding position. By geometry, I mean the angles the seat tube, head tube and forks make with horizontal. Touring and mixte frames most likely had gears initially, but they will still be great for turning into a single-speed for city riding. Although it's subtle, as you can see in the pictures below, the shallower the angles, the more upright the rider. There is nothing wrong with this – in fact, upright is a great position for those who commute around town, like the Dutch do. You're able to see above traffic, and have almost a 180-degree view. You'll also notice the fork has more 'rake', ie its curve forward – this is the offset of the fork dropouts to produce a longer wheelbase, creating more stability and control for the rider.

When the angles get steeper, it makes a more aggressive position, as in a track or road frame. Again, there's nothing wrong with this, but it should be used in the right context. It makes the rider more aerodynamic and gives better power transfer from pedalling. Not a great position to be in while in traffic, but absolutely wonderful when riding down country lanes.

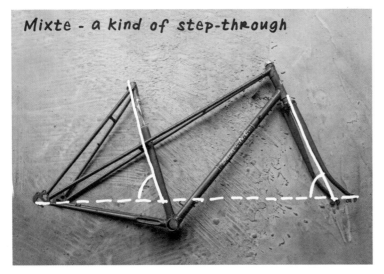

Mixte - a kind of step-through

Track

Touring

AND NOW, A QUIZ!

What are you going to use your bike for?

A Commuting

B Road/track riding

C Touring

D Going off dirt jumps and berms

E Pootling about

F Transporting goods/children

G A mix of things

If you answered A or E, you should find a frame with shallower angles that is fairly upright so that you can see traffic, as in the step-through or touring frames we mentioned on the previous page.

If B was your choice, you can go for a more steep geometry, as with a track frame.

If you said C, get a frame that's angled in between A and B.

If it's D, mountain bike frames are made for you.

If you answered F, you'll be looking for an upright frame as well so that you'll have more control while hauling precious cargo.

If you chose G, try to find a frame that's in between your choices – but remember, there are different types of bikes for different types of rides. It'll give you a good excuse to build more than one…

In this book, I'll be covering how to put together a single-speed bicycle, and this can apply to A, B, E and sometimes D. You can apply this to C, but it's not recommended, as while touring you'll usually be carrying lots of weight and going up/down hills – but not always! If you're 'credit-card touring' (ie sleeping in B&Bs) through Holland, for instance, by all means build a single-speed touring bike. Likewise with F, you can have a single-speed cargo bike, but due to heavy loads you're gonna really appreciate some gears on there.

CHOOSING A FRAME THAT FITS YOU

Bike fit

We're not talking professional bike fitting here – we'll leave that to the pros. But you should have a general idea of what size of bike you should be riding. Most of what I'll be referring to here will apply to vintage bike frames. With modern frames that have compact geometry, there's a whole slew of different methods of measuring, and you can find more info online. Here's a handy chart based on height.

Determining your road bike frame size		
Height	**Inseam length**	**Bike frame size**
147 – 155cm	63 – 69cm	46 – 48cm
152 – 160cm	66 – 71cm	48 – 50cm
157 – 165cm	69 – 74cm	50 – 52cm
163 – 170cm	71 – 76cm	52 – 54cm
168 – 175cm	74 – 79cm	54 – 56cm
173 – 180cm	76 – 81cm	56 – 58cm
178 – 185cm	81 – 84cm	58 – 60cm
183 – 190cm	84 – 86cm	60 – 62cm
188 – 196cm	86 – 91cm	62 – 64cm

MEASURING A BIKE FRAME

To know what size your frame is, measure the top tube and seat tube. The top tube is the one that goes across the top of the frame connecting the head tube and seat tube, and the seat tube is the one that goes down from the seatpost to the bottom-bracket shell. On vintage frames, this measurement is fairly straightforward, thanks to a perfectly horizontal top tube.

1 Measure the top tube
Start at the *centre* of the head tube, and end at the *centre* of the seat tube, ensuring horizontal measurement.

2 Measure the seat tube
Start at the top of the seat tube and end at the centre of the bottom-bracket shell.

If you're using a step-through frame, use a straight object to measure a horizontal line from the centre of the head tube to the centre of the seatpost. From this point measure to the centre of the bottom bracket shell. These are the 'effective' top tube and seat tube measurements.

These two measurements are important to note when taking into consideration what size of bike you need. Even if the size is officially a 52cm, it doesn't mean it's actually 52cm across and 52cm down. Take into consideration your body here. If you have a short torso and long legs (like me), you'll want a bike with a shorter top tube and longer seat tube, or at least a 'square' frame, where both measurements are equal.

You can make up the difference with a longer seat post, shorter stem, and/or swept-back bars. Unfortunately for me, a lot of vintage racers have the opposite

measurements, where the top tube is longer than the seat tube – but this is great for people with longer torsos and shorter legs.

If the frame has wheels attached, another way to check if the size will suit you is to stand over the top tube. It should be 1" away from your bits. Too close and the frame is too big, more than 2" away and the frame is too small.

If you can, take it for a ride as well, and see how it feels. A too-short stem/top-tube length will make for a 'twitchy' ride feel, too long and you'll feel stretched out.

FRAME ESSENTIALS

New frames

Look for single-speed specific frames. These will be made with (usually) 120mm spacing on the rear dropouts, ensuring a rear single-speed wheel will fit in your frame. For this particular bike we'll be building, you'll need a bike with a 1" head tube as well.

Used frames

Most vintage frames can be converted into single-speed bikes fairly easily, but you'll need to look for a few specific features.

• Semi-horizontal dropouts – this will allow you to pull your wheel back to get the right chain tension. Vertical dropouts will not allow this, and you'll have to install a chain tensioner. If this is the case, then look for a bike with a mech hanger that will allow for a chain tensioner to be installed. As a general rule, bikes with vertical dropouts cannot be made into fixed gear bikes.
• Horizontal 'fork ends' (technically they're not dropouts because the wheel doesn't 'drop out') are also fine. These are most often found on track-specific frames.

Semi-horizontal dropouts

Horizontal fork ends

- Rear dropout spacing should be between 110mm and 126mm. If you have a steel frame (to test for this, put a magnet on it – if it sticks, it's steel), you have some flexibility with the spacing and can pull the stays to fit a single-speed wheel.
- A 1" head tube: we'll be building with a quill stem, which requires a 1" headset to go in the head tube.
- Threaded fork: for the aforementioned headset, we'll need a 1" threaded fork.
- Drilled for caliper brakes. Your bike will need holes in the fork and the rear brake bridge to take a set of rim brakes.

Is this frame safe to ride?

The problem with a used frame is that you don't know its history. A crash can cause subtle but serious damage. Perhaps you may be the second owner of the bike and the first was your mum – she may not remember the time she lent the bike to your uncle who crashed it but didn't tell anyone, and he carries this dark secret with him to this day. Have a conversation with the owner to find out more of the bike's history, or purchase from a reputable secondhand dealer.

Here are a few danger signs to watch out for when looking for a secondhand frame:
- Bent forks: either the steerer is bent, or the fork arms are bent. It could have been caused by a front or side crash.
- Bent frame: top tube/down tube bulges on the underside by the head tube; rear dropouts bent/out of alignment; ovalised seat tube or head tube.
- Cracks – look around the tube joins, especially between the head tube and top tube, and on the bottom bracket.
- Worn threading in the bottom bracket or fork steerer tube.

Side-on collision

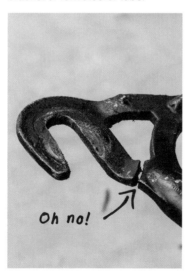

Oh no!

Cracked frame

THE 'M-CHECK'

In the workshop I use something called the M-check, so called because it's done in the shape of an 'M' on the bike. Here's an M-check list to use when inspecting a bike before you buy. All the things here indicate signs of wear, and should be either serviced or replaced.

Front wheel

- Hub: check for play by moving the wheel side to side (the way it's not supposed to move) by holding the fork arm or seat stay with one hand and the wheel in the other. Spin to see how the bearings feel. Do they spin for a while or slow down quickly? Do they feel grindy, like some grit or dirt is in the hub?
- Spokes: check to see if any are loose or broken by giving them a gentle squeeze. They should give a tiny bit, but not loads.
- Rim: check for concavity and wear by feeling the side of the rim. It should be straight up and down, and not curved in towards the centre of the rim. Also check for any damage – major scratches or dings. Spin the wheel and look at the gap between the brake pad and rim – any wiggle means the wheel isn't true (straight).
- Tyres: check for wear, tears, cracks, holes, and puncture-causing objects like glass, thorns or tacks.

Front brake

- Pads: check for wear – you want to see the grooves or 'teeth'. If the pad is totally flat, or worse – showing metal – you'll need new ones. Hopefully it hasn't damaged the rim!
- Brake calipers: do they work? Do they open and close evenly or does one side stick?

Saddle/seatpost

- A saddle is easy to change, so don't worry if it doesn't look great.
- Ideally, make sure that the seatpost isn't stuck in the frame. For more details on removing stuck seatposts, see p46.

Drivetrain

- Pedals: check for play. Hold one with both hands and try to move it the way it shouldn't move – don't spin it around, but move it up and down. If there is movement, aka 'knocking', you might want to replace them. It could become a source of annoying clicks.
- Bottom bracket: check for play. Hold one crank arm in each hand and rock them in and out towards the frame – not round and round. If both crank arms move in the same direction and produce a 'knocking' feeling, the bottom bracket is loose and should be either serviced or replaced. If only one arm moves, then it's the crank arm that is loose, and *not* the bottom bracket.
- Chain: is it clean? Check for wear with a chain wear indicator. If the tooth drops in at 0.75% wear, you need to replace the chain. If it drops in at 1% wear, you'll need to replace the chain, freewheel and possibly the chainring. (If it has multiple gears, don't worry even if it's worn out – you'll be replacing the wheel.) If you don't have a chain wear indicator handy, you can use a ruler. Pins on a new chain are always ½" from each other. Start the ruler at the centre of one pin, then look five to ten inches down the length. If the chain pins start to fall out of sync with the ruler, you need a new chain.
- Chainring: check for 'shark-toothing', where the chainring teeth are so worn they're super-pointy.

Headset

- Check for play by holding the front brake lever down, and

Check saddle and seatpost

Check cockpit

Check brakes

Check wheel

Check frame

Check wheel

Check drivetrain

pushing the bike forward and back. You can also hold the fork in one hand and the head tube in the other, and move them away from each other, in the direction they're not meant to go. Is there a 'knocking' feeling? Check for tightness/wear by picking up the front end of the bike and allowing the wheel to flop to the side. Does it do so easily, or does it slow down? Check for 'indexing', where the bearings have become bedded into the headset cup, by picking up the front end of the bike 1cm off the ground, gently nudging the front wheel to the side, and seeing if it keeps moving to the side. If it springs back to the centre, the headset is indexed and should be replaced. The headset may also feel too tight, or grindy/sandy. When you pick up the front end of the bike and the handlebars don't flop easily side to side, the headset is too tight and needs to be serviced, or even replaced.

Stem

• Check for cracks, especially near the handlebar clamp. If the frame is old, check if the stem is stuck. Unscrew the stem bolt about 1cm. Then hit it once with a hammer. If it doesn't drop in, the wedge or stem may be stuck. If it does drop in, proceed to twist the bars from the fork. It should come undone fairly easily. If it doesn't, try using GT85 or PlusGas to remove it, but you need to consider if you have the time and energy to take it out yourself, or money to spend to get it taken out by a pro. See p46 on how to take out a stuck stem – it's a similar method to taking out a stuck seatpost.

Handlebars

• Are they straight and in alignment with the frame, or are they wonky or bent?

Brake levers

• Do they work? Do they spring back quickly after you let go of the lever?

Brake cables

• Are they exposed? Rusted? Do they feel 'gritty' when you brake?

Fork

• Is it bent? Forks that have been in a crash will be pushed backwards in a head-on collision, or a side collision could push the arms out of alignment.

Frame

• As mentioned on p35, try to make sure it hasn't been in a serious crash. Check the joins between the head tube and top tube/down tube – bulges on the underside and/or cracks on the top are a sign there has been a head-on collision.
• Check if the rear stays are in alignment with the rest of the frame by tying a string to one dropout. Bring the string to the front of the frame and around the head tube, and tie it back on to the other dropout. Measure the distance between the seat tube and string on both sides. They should be equal. If they are not, the rear triangle is out of alignment. If the frame is steel, it may be possible to 'cold set' it (bend it) – but take it to your local bike shop or DIY workshop to do this.

Rear brake

• Check as with the front brake.

Rear wheel

• Check as with the front wheel.
• Freewheel: check the condition of the freewheel. If the chain wear indicator said 1% wear, then you should change it to a new one.

GETTING YOUR FRAME

Armed with this information, you are now ready to charge headfirst into the dizzying world of frame buying! I absolutely insist that you see a secondhand frame in person before you buy it. You need to be able to inspect it for damage, and ask the owner questions about its past. If it seems too good to be true, it probably is.

Where to buy a secondhand frame

Best bet is to start with your local community bike project. They will usually have good deals and can help answer questions. Other great places to check out are specialist vintage bike shops, bike jumble sales, and your family and friends.

If you want to search online, that's fine, but know the risks: you can't see the frame, the bike could get damaged during shipping, the measurements could be off, or the seller could be straight-up lying (all these things have happened to people I know). If you're buying online, try to see the frame before any transaction happens.

Whatever you do, do not buy a stolen bike. A whole heap of bad karma will be heading your way if you do. Here are some giveaways

that the bike is hot, and not in a good way:

- The price seems incredibly cheap
- The seller seems like they want to sell the bike as quickly as possible
- They won't meet you in a public place
- They won't provide a receipt confirming payment
- They want cash only
- They won't provide you with a frame number that you can check against a stolen bike database

Enjoy your time at this point and don't rush. Getting to choose a frame is a privilege and an exciting experience. Savour it.

TAKING YOUR BIKE APART

If you've got yourself a secondhand frame,
there may be loads of bike bits attached to
it that will have to be taken off. Don't panic! In
this section I'll cover how to strip that frame
as bare as the day it was born. You'll end up with
a neat pile of parts, some of which may be able
to be reused. You may not have to do these steps,
so read through and see which ones apply to you.
Bonus: you'll also end up with a clearer idea of
how a bicycle works - which will help you rebuild.

GATHER THESE TOOLS

- [ ] Workstand
- [ ] Hex key set up to 8mm
- [ ] Spanner set 8mm-17mm
- [ ] 14mm socket
- [ ] Adjustable spanner (at least 32mm)
- [ ] Hammer and punch
- [ ] Pedal spanner
- [ ] Tyre levers
- [ ] Crank extractor
- [ ] 1" headcup remover
- [ ] Cable cutters
- [ ] Chainbreaker
- [ ] Pliers
- [ ] Screwdrivers
    - flathead and crosshead (Phillips)
- [ ] PlusGas (hopefully not)
- [ ] Freewheel remover (possibly)

Hex keys vs adjustable spanners
The tools you need will depend on what parts are on your bike. Older frames may not require hex keys, and newer frames may not require spanners, but to be safe, I'm listing all the tools here. Look at the fixings on your bike and see which you require – might be both! And, a quick word on adjustable spanners. They're never the wrong size and never the right size. They can slip while in use because of this, and this can round out nuts, rendering them useless. I can tell when someone's been using one, I'm like a dentist in that way. Use the correctly sized spanner.

...AND GET A BOTTOM BRACKET TOOL

You'll definitely need one of these, but which one will depend on what type of bottom bracket you have. The picture below shows parts of bottom brackets and their respective tools.

Adjustable bottom brackets

These are made up of four pieces: an adjustable cup, a fixed cup, a spindle and a lockring. You'll need an adjustable cup spanner that matches the shape of your particular adjustable cup, and a fixed cup spanner.

Square-taper bottom brackets

These consist of a large cartridge with threads on one side and a separate threaded cup on the other. You will need a BB tool that fits into the shape of your cup, and possibly a retaining bolt to make sure it doesn't slip.

External bottom bracket

It's slightly possible you might have one of these, but I will not be covering them. For removal I recommend going to your local bike shop and getting a pro to do it.

Cottered cranks

These are made up of an adjustable cup, a fixed cup, a spindle, a lockring and two cotter pins. While there's nothing inherently wrong with cottered crank technology (it has lasted for decades), if the cranks are loose, I recommend switching to a square-taper sealed bottom bracket for your new build. Cotter pins are not what they used to be – they tend to be made of toffee these days, and the cranks will come loose a lot quicker, destroying the pins. Get a pro to do it for you for a small fee.

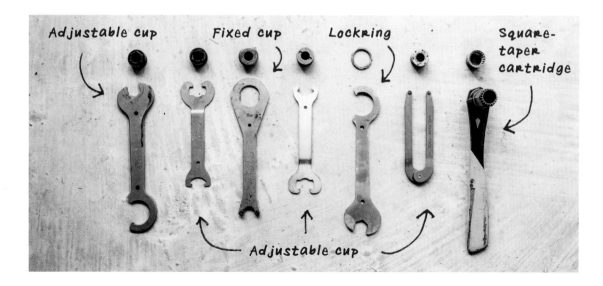

Adjustable cup Fixed cup Lockring Square-taper cartridge Adjustable cup

TIME TO TAKE IT ALL OFF

01

Mount it in the workstand
We're going to remove all the parts from your secondhand bike, and just leave us with a frame and fork. It may well be that you'd like to reuse some of the parts – great! Just make sure you don't lose any small bits. It's a good idea to take photos along the way so you can remember the order parts have come off in.

• Put the bike in the workstand, drive-side (the one with the chain) facing out. Clamp around the seat tube. You *can* clamp around the seatpost, but if it's carbon don't do it too tight. If the frame has nice paint, use a rag to protect it and tighten the clamp so it's secure but not mega tight.

• If you don't have a workstand, flip the bike upside down.

Make sure the seatpost isn't stuck

• Undo the seat bolt and remove the seatpost and saddle. If it doesn't move, chances are there has been a reaction between the seatpost and frame. If they're both made of steel (older seatposts sometimes are), they could be rusted together. (This information can also apply to quill stems.) If it's an alloy seatpost and a steel frame, there could be corrosion or even bonding of metals. But there are a couple of things you can do to try to get it out yourself.

• Drizzle some GT85 or PlusGas in between the seatpost and frame. Tap the seatpost gently with a hammer to try to get the liquid to sneak in further. One of our mechanics repeated this every single day for a few weeks, and was finally successful.

• Use a sacrificial saddle as a lever to twist the seatpost back and forth out of the frame (the saddle may not survive this).

• If you have a giant vice handy, you can turn the bicycle upside down, clamp the seatpost or saddle in its jaws, and use the frame for extra leverage. But you probably don't have a giant vice because you're a normal person. So if it's not budging, you'll need to take it to a bike shop to get it taken out. They may apply heat to the tube.

• Another option is to take it to a workshop or metalworks that does powder coating. They will have large ovens to heat up your bike. An alloy seatpost will melt before a steel frame, but this process will take off paint. This is pretty much the final option, but almost always works – worth it if you have a sweet frame you don't want to give up on!

• And if you go through all this, it will be the ultimate lesson – prevent this from happening in the future by liberally applying grease in the seat tube on a regular basis.

O2

Remove the wheels
- Take them off with a spanner if they have nuts, or by undoing the quick-release lever.
- If you have a quick-release, pull the lever away from the frame, and then unscrew the nut from the opposite side. Both nuts and quick-release just have to be loose to get the wheel off the frame, they don't have to come off completely.
- You may need to deflate the tyre to get it out of the brake arms.

Remove the tyres

- I like to take off a tyre with two tyre levers at the same time (it's faster). Start opposite the valve, and line up the tyre lever with one of the spokes.
- Place the scoop end underneath the rim (aka bead) of the tyre. On the same side, line up the second lever on the next spoke over and place the scoop end under the bead.
- Push down on both levers and hook one around a spoke. Use the second lever to peel the tyre bead off, keeping it parallel with the wheel rim.
- Pull the tube out, and then using brute force, pull the tyre up and over the rim.
- If you're reusing the wheel take note of the condition of the rim tape, and if it needs to be replaced (see p125).

04

Remove the freewheel/ fixed sprocket

• Use the correctly shaped freewheel remover. Place the tool in the holes on the freewheel, and turn left to undo with an adjustable spanner. If it's tough, you may need PlusGas and a vice. Be aware of cheap freewheels that don't have holes for a remover – these will need to be crushed in a vice. Promise me you will *not* use one of these on your new bike! They are awful.

• To remove a fixed sprocket, use a lockring spanner to undo the lockring first – this is reverse thread, so turn right to undo.

• Once that's off, use a chain whip to undo the sprocket. This is regular thread, so turn left to undo. Wrap the chain around the sprocket and push down.

05

Disconnect the cables

- Cut off any cable end caps at the brake calipers or derailleurs with a cable cutter.
- To disconnect cables, use a hex key (probably 5mm) or spanner (probably 10mm). Locate where the cable is being pinched on brakes and gears, and loosen the bolt.

Ob

Remove the brake calipers
- Using either a spanner or hex key, unscrew the nut holding the brake to the frame. There may be an arrangement of nuts and washers holding it on – if you're reusing them remember the order by taking pictures or making sketches.

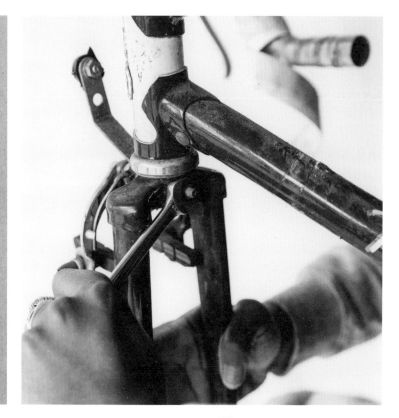

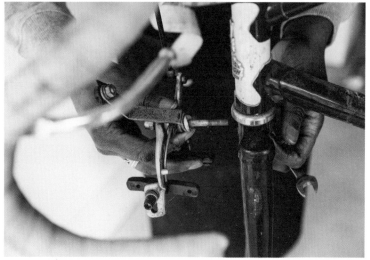

07

Remove the chain

If there is a quick link somewhere in the chain, you won't need a chainbreaker. What's a quick link? Well…

Single-speed quick links

• Two-piece single speed quick link posts will need bending towards each other in order to pop the front plate off.

• If they are three-piece single-speed quick links, slide off the outer clip with a pair of pliers, then remove the outer plate from the pins.

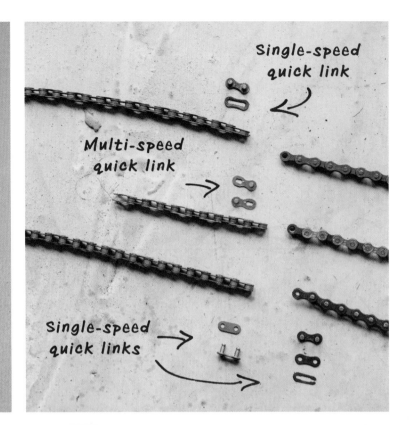

Single-speed quick link

Multi-speed quick link

Single-speed quick links

Multi-speed quick links

- If they look like they have a small hole in the middle of the outer plate on either side, sometimes you can just slide the two sides in towards each other, so that the pins move towards the larger hole in the side plate.
- If this doesn't work, you'll need quick-link-specific pliers, or just use a chainbreaker.

Using a chainbreaker

- If you don't have a quick link at all, you'll be using a chainbreaker. It's best to proceed slowly and carefully when breaking a chain.
- If you have a single-speed chain, you need a chainbreaker that can fit a single-speed chain.
- If you have a multi-speed chain, make sure your chainbreaker can accommodate that size of chain.
- Choose any pin on the chain. I prefer one on the bottom so that the chain won't fly open when the tension is released.
- Place the teeth from the chain tool around the pin you're removing. Make sure the pin from the tool is lined up with the pin from the chain, hold it in place with your thumb, then turn the handle on the chain tool. This will push out the pin from the chain.
- You'll need to use The Force: use your feelings and your sight to gauge where the pin is. It will be harder pushing the pin through the inner and outer plates, easier when the pin goes through the middle, and it gets hard again when it reaches the other two plates.
- At this point, stop, back off, remove the tool and take one side of the chain in each hand.
- Bend the link towards you, like you want to snap it in half.
- If it doesn't break, give the chain tool a quarter-turn to push the pin out a bit more, keeping a careful eye to make sure the pin doesn't go too far out. Try breaking the chain again.
- Repeat this process until the chain comes apart. If the pin comes all the way out, that's okay too.
- If you're reusing the chain, you should reconnect it with a quick link, but if you have no choice, you can push the pin back through. If the pin has come out completely, it's impossible to put back – trust me.

Remove the handlebars

If you're reusing the handlebars but not the quill stem, it's easier to remove the handlebars at this point.

• Remove whatever's on the bar (ie unwrapping bar tape, unscrewing brake lever, bell etc) on one side. Loosen the bolt that's clamped around the handlebar centre to slide the bar out.

• If you're changing the levers (the bits you pull to make it stop!), remove them both by unscrewing them from the handlebars. If you have drop bar levers, you'll most likely need to press the lever down to expose the bolt, then unscrew it.

• Drop (racing) bars have a couple of curves that have to be swivelled around. Keep the inner part of the curve where the stem clamp is narrower and it'll be a lot easier to remove.

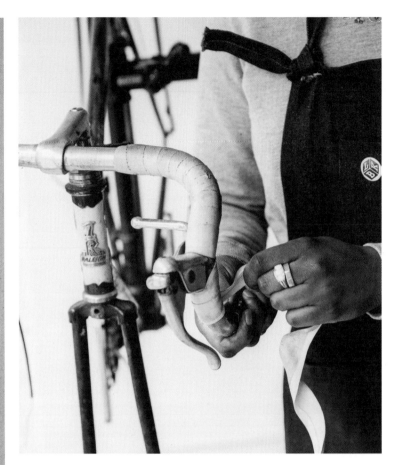

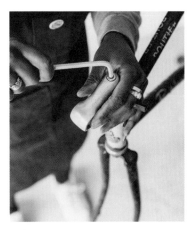

09

Remove the quill stem

• Use the correct hex key (probably 6mm) or spanner, and unscrew the stem bolt 1cm from the stem. (The handlebars could still be attached, if you plan to reuse them *and* the stem.)

• Don't unscrew it all the way! Use a hammer on the hex key to whack the bolt back down into the stem. Give it a good tap. This will dislodge the wedge from the stem and allow you to wiggle it out of the fork steerer tube.

• Use the handlebars, if they're still attached, as leverage and twist it separately from the fork. If it's stuck see p46.

10

Remove the headset
• Use a headset spanner and/or an adjustable spanner to unscrew the top locknut from the adjustable race. (See p17 for a handy diagram of an exploded headset.)
• Keep hold of the fork so it doesn't fall on the ground, and unscrew both the locknut and race from the fork steerer tube. Remove the bearings and any seals, then finally slide out the fork.
• If the whole headset seems in good condition, you can reuse it. Just replace bearings – loose or caged – with new ones.

Headset cup removal

You'll need a 1" headcup removal tool and a hammer. Insert it closed-end first into the headset tube from the bottom to the top. You'll hear it click when it's in place.

• Place a rag on the bottom cup and hold it there with one hand. With your other hand firmly hit the top of the tool with the hammer until the cup comes out. Don't let the tool fall to the ground!

• Repeat this on the opposite cup – either flip the frame around so that you're hitting the headcup remover from the top again, or insert the tool from the top to the bottom of the head tube until you hear a click. Then hit the closed end of the tool from the bottom up.

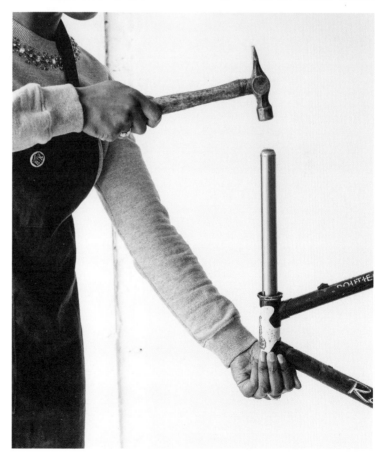

Remove the crown race from the fork crown

• Turn the fork upside down, place the fork steerer tube (preferably) on a forgiving surface like wood, and lean it against a wall. This will prevent any damage to the steerer tube while you're tapping away.

• Using a hammer and punch, gently tap the edges of the crown race away from the fork crown. Work your way around until it comes off.

11

Remove the derailleurs
If they're present, that is (they won't be if the bike is already single-speed or fixed gear).
• Using either a spanner or hex key, unscrew the bolt holding the derailleur to the frame.

12

Remove the pedals

- When unscrewing, pedals loosen going towards the back of the bike, so there's a regular thread on the drive-side and reverse thread on the non-drive-side – righty loosey.
- An easy way of doing this is to position the crank arm going forward towards the front of the bike, and the 15mm spanner or 6mm hex key pointing towards the back.
- Push the pedal down in one hand and the spanner with the other. Repeat on both sides.

13

Remove the cranks

Removing cranks is like opening a wine bottle. It's a two-step process where you screw in one part first, and then the second step pulls out the cork – I mean, crank.

- Unscrew or pop off any plastic crank bolt cover.
- Using a 14mm socket or 8mm hex key, unscrew the crank bolts on both sides. Remove any washers that may be inside. (If you don't, you may destroy your cranks in the next stage.)

- Carefully screw the outer portion of the crank extractor into the threads of the crank. Make sure it's going in straight, it's going in easy, and you're not forcing it. Don't use any tools at this point: you should be able to do it by hand. Screw it in as far as it will go, then tighten a little with a 15mm spanner. If it doesn't go, do not force it in. It could be that the threads are damaged, or you have a weird Stronglight or TA crankset, which requires a different extractor thread pitch and diameter. If this is the case, seek professional help.
- Now screw in the second part of the tool, either with its own handle if it has one, or with a spanner if it doesn't.

It will turn easily until the point where it hits the bottom bracket spindle. When this happens, you have to keep going – this is the extraction part of the process. It may be difficult, you may want to give up, but don't! Keep applying pressure. Remember that you have more power pushing down. If it's really tough, add some leverage to the handle in the form of a metal tube that can go over the handle, or get a second pair of hands to help you out here. Once it gets easy again, the crank should come straight off. Just pull it towards you.
- Unscrew the tool and repeat on the other side.

14

Remove the bottom bracket

• If it's an adjustable bottom bracket, using a lockring spanner, unscrew the lockring from the non-drive-side of the bike. You can also use a hammer and punch – place the punch on one of the teeth on the left side of the lockring and gently tap it an the anticlockwise direction.

• Then, using the appropriately shaped tool, unscrew the adjustable cup. The spindle and bearings will come out too at this point.

• Now remove the fixed cup – this is where it gets specialised: If you have a British thread frame (most modern makes) the threads will be reversed. Turn clockwise to loosen. If it's old French or Italian, it may need to be turned counterclockwise. If you're not sure, try both ways. (For more on bottom brackets, see p90.) Make a note of what kind of bottom bracket you have; if you need a new one, it will have to be compatible with the threads on the frame.

- Or, is it a sealed cartridge bottom bracket? These modern beauties are systems where the bearings are sealed inside. They are advantageous in two ways. Firstly, because the bearings and grease are kept inside, they stay cleaner for longer. And cleaner means less dirt and grit grinding down your cups, spindle and bearings.

Secondly, they just slot right in and are ready to use. No need to perform a fancy balancing act to get the sweet spot where it's not too tight and not too loose. (A disadvantage will be their slightly larger weight and the fact they can't be serviced.)

- For removal you will need a sealed cartridge bottom bracket tool. Start with the non-drive-side of the bike. Position the tool firmly in the splines of the cup. Unscrew anticlockwise to remove. A single cup will come out on this side.

- Repeat on the drive-side, turning clockwise if you have a British threaded bottom bracket shell, or anticlockwise if you have an Italian/French bottom bracket shell. The full cartridge will come out on this side.

Troubleshooting

If you struggle here, there are fixes.

- Lay the bike on its side and dribble a little GT85 or PlusGas between the threads of the cup and frame. Let it soak in for a bit then try removing it again.
- Use a hammer to tap the bottom bracket tool gently in the direction it should be unscrewing – you're trying to 'shake up and wake up' the threads. If you're still struggling, you can keep applying PlusGas and using the tool on the cup for a few days. If after this point it's still not budging, best to take it to a bike shop. They will have a variety of hench tools to pull it out.
- It may be that the cup is really stuck in there. In this instance, a retaining bolt will help keep the tool inside the cup, and you can push down as hard as you like. Pedro's makes an excellent retaining bolt.
- Once the cup moves, stop immediately and unscrew the retaining bolt. If you don't, the tool can jam between the cup and retaining bolt and you won't be able to unscrew any further.

67

15

Prepare the frame

When you've got the frame and fork all on its own, here's a chance to make it even more your own. That might be as simple as giving it a good clean with a brush and detergent or rubbing alcohol, or you can go further – paint it. You can go minimal by simply choosing your favourite colour, or get deep customisation if you've got the budget for it. But any which way you choose to do it, you'll end up with a bike that's a bit more bespoke.

On the next page there's an overview of available methods, but it's definitely not comprehensive! There are loads of different tutorials online and, of course, differing opinions. Here I am talking about working with a steel frame. I would recommend doing research before proceeding, especially if your frame is aluminium, carbon or titanium.

If you're going to be painting your frame, the first thing you should do is remove whatever's on it at the moment. Previous paint jobs won't allow new paint to completely stick, unless that's the vibe you're going for, which is totally fine too. But if you want to go fully fresh and clean, start by cleaning up the frame.

Touch up

If you like the colour of your frame, but it's got a few nicks and bits of paint missing, the easiest way to remedy this is nail varnish. It comes in thousands of colours, you can find it at the local pharmacy, and it's cheap. You might feel a bit awkward taking your frame to the shop to match it, but whatevs – do it for the sake of your bike.

Stickers

Stickers are a great way to personalise your bike – think of all the rad people who have given you rad stickers, and put them on your bike! They make it completely yours, and could make it less attractive to thieves (who probably don't want a bike that's easily recognisable). There are vinyl sticker kits that cover your entire frame, and there are even stickers that 'uglify' your bike – they look like rust and dings and scratches, oh my…

Removing decals

If the original manufacturer decals aren't under a coat of lacquer, you can easily take them off. Be sure to take a photo if you want to put new ones on that are exactly the same later on. Heat up the area with a hairdryer to loosen the adhesive and scrape off the decal with an old credit card. There may be some other tiny bits left – you can use a dull utility knife blade for these, but be careful not to scrape the paint off. You can also use a chemical adhesive remover, like Goo Gone, to help get the last bits off. Beware that nail varnish remover may take off paint, so avoid at all costs.

Removing paint – DIY

This is quite an involved and hazardous process, and there's not enough room for me to explain everything, so I recommend visiting ye olde internet for this one. But basically you'd use a chemical paint stripper, which is highly toxic. If you go down this route, remember to wear proper protective equipment.

Removing rust – DIY

There are several ways of removing superficial rust from a frame. Naval Jelly, oil and steel wool, or even lime juice and steel wool are just a few methods. If the rust has become so bad that there's structural damage (ie holes!) then you're gonna have to get it repaired by a professional, or even consider getting a new frame.

Media blasting

If DIY removal is proving a pain, if you don't have the time, or if you want a really thorough job done, get it blasted (this could be sand or glass bead blasting). I totally recommend this. It's a quick and clean process done by a professional, where they blast your frame with a very fine abrasive to get every single bit of whatever's not originally part of the frame off. It's not expensive and it can be done quickly – a non-bike-specific workshop will be cheaper. Just touch it as little as possible once it's done, as the natural oils and dirt from your hands can ruin the upcoming paint job.

Paint the frame

You'll need to protect certain parts of the bike before you start painting. Put old bottom bracket cups halfway through, wrap masking or duct tape around the cups and then screw in a bit more – this will protect your threads. Put in some old headset cups and a seatpost to protect the inside of your head tube and seat tube.

Primer

Always start with a primer coat. This will protect the frame from rust and corrosion when the inevitable chipping occurs. It'll also help subsequent coats of paint to adhere. You can use putty to fill in minor dings.

DIY painting

Use spray paint, or a specific bicycle frame spray paint (like SprayBike). SprayBike is like a combination between powder coating and spray paint, so there's less dripping. You can also use a brush with enamel paint – it's easier and less hazardous but doesn't give an even finish like spraying does.

DIY drawing

Another option here is to use a marker pen to draw all over your frame once it's painted. Get your friend's kids to draw on it. Barter with a stranger or pay a local tattoo artist. It'll be a totally unique and memorable experience in addition to being a totally unique bike.

Topcoat

A marine epoxy enamel is a great topcoat after you've painted. If you like the way a raw frame looks, or if you've done the aforementioned drawing, you should finish the frame with a clear topcoat to make sure that it's protected from the elements and the artwork is preserved.

Powder coating

Powder coating isn't a paint. An electrostatic gun sprays charged powder on the frame. It's then put into an oven to melt into a hard-wearing coat. It doesn't use solvents, so it's more environmentally friendly. But the colour will be less dynamic than a wet spray, and actually adds weight.

Wet spray

Painting, or wet spray, employs the same paint that's used on cars. It comes in a mind-boggling selection of finishes and colours, and the combinations are endless. Go glitter, pearlescent, neon, metallic; get finishes like crackle, fades, splatter, prismatic, or glow-in-the-dark. The paint wizards can make your dreams come true.

Hydrographics

Also known as immersion printing and hydro dipping, this a fairly new process to transfer complex images on to 3D surfaces. After a frame is painted it's then dipped into a large vat of water where the image can wrap itself around the frame. It's expensive though, and energy intensive.

Frame finishing

If you've had your frame professionally powder coated or painted, you'll probably need to get the threads chased on your bottom bracket, and the drive-side and head tube will need to be faced. Your local bike shop will be able to do this for you for a small fee.

Insider info: for the frame on the right there, I chose to go with a wet spray to get a lovely metallic sunset orange.

SELECTING COMPONENTS

Now is the time to find the parts with which to build up your bike. At first glance, a bike may seem to be a simple object; but like most simple things, it is anything but. A lot of thought and care will be needed to make sure your build goes smoothly. Pay careful attention when choosing parts and use your budget wisely. In the bike world, cheap parts usually mean poor quality, so get the best you can afford. And, finally - buy from your local bike shop!

WHAT PARTS DO YOU HAVE, WHAT DO YOU NEED TO GET?

- [ ] Frame
- [ ] Forks
- [ ] Wheels
- [ ] Tyres
- [ ] Inner tubes
- [ ] Rim tape
- [ ] Bottom bracket
- [ ] Chainset
- [ ] Pedals
- [ ] Chain
- [ ] Single-speed freewheel
- [ ] Headset
- [ ] Stem

- [ ] Handlebars
- [ ] Brake levers
- [ ] Brake calipers
- [ ] Brake cables
- [ ] Brake housing
- [ ] Housing ferrules
- [ ] Brake pads
- [ ] Cable end caps
- [ ] Seatpost
- [ ] Saddle
- [ ] Seatpost bolt or collar
- [ ] Grips/bartape

WHEN TO REPLACE

If components are cracked, torn, worn or simply busted, they should be replaced. As a general rule, if something is rusty, you should probably replace it. Rust isn't necessarily a sign that something is worn, but it does mean it's been left to fend for itself in the elements, and that can be a sign that something is old and hasn't been taken care of. If you haven't already, go through the M-check (on p36) to determine what parts need to be replaced.

In the transition from old bike to new, I would recommend changing cables, housing, brake pads, chain and tyres. Furthermore, I would consider changing the bottom bracket, crankset, headset and freewheel.

If you see pitting in bearing systems (tiny little dots or sometimes huge gouges) where ball bearings and dirt have been impacting cups and races, replace.

If you see corrosion – rust or white powder – on cables and housing that should be clean and shiny silver, replace.

If you see 'shark toothing' on drivetrain components (very sharp pointed teeth on chainrings and freewheels)… replace!

Shark toothing

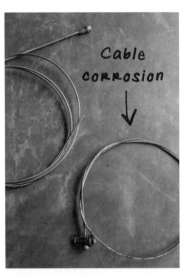

Cable corrosion

Very bad pitting!

WHERE TO GET NEW BIKE PARTS

There's a plethora of sources out there once you know what you're looking for. In the real world, vintage bike shops and community bike spaces sell secondhand parts. There are also bike jumbles, like car boot sales (or swap meets for you Americans) that deal solely in old bike bits. In the internet world, check out eBay or specialist retailers. I'd like to take a moment to discourage you from ordering from the online discount retailers, as they are killing business for the local bike shop (LBS).

The LBS is an endangered species, one that we may not fully appreciate till it's gone. They are fonts of knowledge, businesses that pride themselves on providing good service, dedicated to ensuring that your bike will run smoothly. When something goes wrong with your bike (and things *will* go wrong), and you're wearing your smart work clothes, and you're running late… who's going to replace that brake cable or inner tube for you while you wait? I encourage you to purchase your parts through your LBS. And when you're a patron, they will be more than happy to answer any burning bike questions you may have.

Also, always keep this in mind: what are you going to be using your bike for? Get yourself components that are going to help you achieve this goal. If you're mainly commuting, you're not going to want knobbly tyres. If you're going for short day rides in the countryside, you're not going to need heavy-duty pannier racks.

You'll need to consider budget and aesthetics as well – but never sacrifice safety. Be careful when buying secondhand parts and make sure there's a warranty or a good returns policy. Nice places to start for online window shopping and inspiration are Charlie the Bikemonger, Brick Lane Bikes and Velo Orange.

VITAL STATISTICS

Now's the time to record the details of your bike. These measurements will help you choose replacement parts. Use vernier calipers to be precise (see p23).

01

Measure the bottom bracket shell. The width will tell you what country your bike is from (see p90), and this will make it easier to determine what type of threading the bottom bracket has.

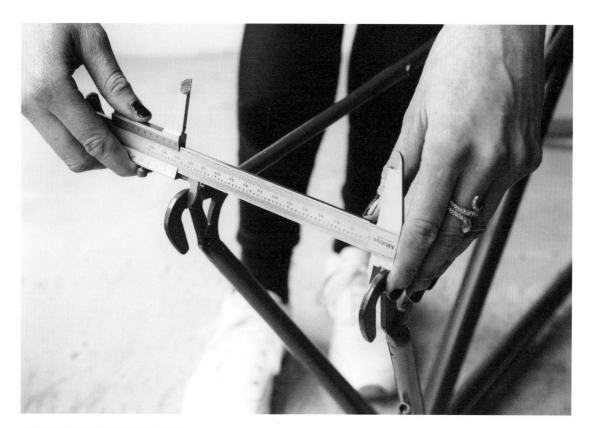

02

Measure the rear dropout spacing from the inside of the frame, and the fork dropout spacing from the inside of the forks. This is to ensure new wheel hubs will fit your frame.

....

....

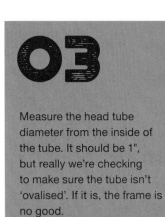

03

Measure the head tube diameter from the inside of the tube. It should be 1", but really we're checking to make sure the tube isn't 'ovalised'. If it is, the frame is no good.

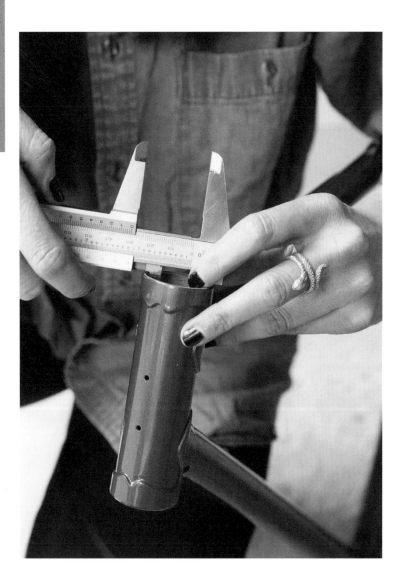

04

Measure the seat tube diameter from the inside of the tube. Older frames can have deformed tubes thanks to a previous owner using the wrong-sized seatpost at some point, so take a couple of different readings at different positions and find the average. Some bike workshops have Stein sizing rods that can help you measure this too.

....

....

FRAME & FORKS

Try to obtain items in this order. Some parts will lead naturally to the next, meaning you'll have the right measurements to keep going.

Frame
This is covered in the chapter Choosing Your Frame.

Fork
If your bike already came with a fork, you're all set. If not, for this book you'll need a 1" threaded fork. Make sure the steerer tube (1 in the picture below) is long enough to accommodate the frame's head tube (2), with a few centimetres

above to fit a headset. To be sure, measure the headset's stack height (see right) and compare with the fork's available stack height. The headset stack height should be a couple of millimetres taller than the available stack height.

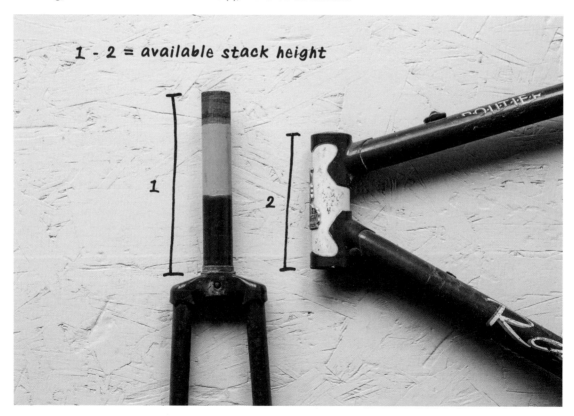

1 - 2 = available stack height

1 Measure the length of the fork steerer tube from the flat bit of the fork crown where the crown race sits (the bottom piece of the headset) to the top of the tube. See p97 for a headset diagram.
2 Measure the length of the frame's head tube from top to bottom.
3 Subtract 2 from 1.

The result is your fork's available stack height. If the headset has exactly the same stack height as your answer, you risk not being able to adjust it well, so in practice you need your headset to be a millimetre or two more than your result. If the fork steerer tube is too long, you can use spacers to take up a few millimetres of extra space; any longer and you'll need to cut the steerer tube down. If you don't have a saw guide and hacksaw to do this, visit your local DIY workshop or LBS. The shortest stack-height headset is the Tange Passage, coming in at 30.22mm. If the fork steerer tube is too short, then – bad news – you need a new fork.

Here's the second fork measurement you will have to know: it needs arms long enough

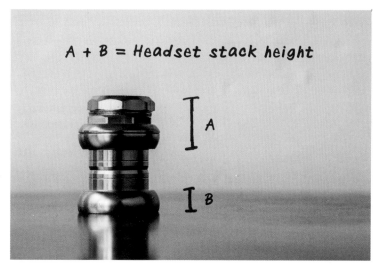

A + B = Headset stack height

to accommodate your front wheel. Use the internet to search the make, model and decade of your bike. You should be able to find bikes with similar specifications, which will list the size of the wheel used. (I go into wheel sizes in more detail on the next page.) Once you know what size of wheel you should use, you can find a fork that will both fit your frame and wheel. If you're using 700c wheels, make sure you get a fork that can take 700c wheels. If you're using a mountain bike frame, you'll likely need 26" wheels and matching-sized fork.

Also, take note of how your brakes will be set up. I will be showing you how to install a caliper brake (p136), which requires the fork crown to be drilled in the front and back for the bolt to go through. If the hole in the back of the fork is 6mm in diameter you'll need to use a nutted vintage brake caliper. If the hole is 8mm you'll be able to use a modern brake caliper with a recessed nut. If the fork has bosses (1" pegs that stick out of your fork arms on both sides), those are for V-brakes or cantilever brakes, and I won't be covering these in this book.

WHEELS

You'll need a front and a rear wheel for your bike, preferably with solid axles (ie, not quick-release). But what size of wheel? Well, since we've sorted the fork side of things, the frameset will now dictate what size and type of wheels to get. If your frame already came with wheels, great! Best to use the same ones, or at least the same size. If your old wheel is a geared one, remember we're changing this bike to a single-speed, so you'll need to get a new, or at least new-to-you, single-speed rear wheel. Unfortunately, back in the day, there was no standardisation of sizes, and your frame may have a rare or even obsolete size. In that case you'll have to find something close enough. It can work!

A brief insight into wheel/tyre/ tube sizing

Because of the lack of standardisation over the years, the European Tyre and Rim Technical Organisation created an internationally recognised standard in 1964, the ETRTO number. This tied together different countries' and manufacturers' sizing into a widely used system.

ERTRO numbers are metric measurements of widths and diameters. On a tyre, it consists of two numbers: the first is double-digit and refers to width, and the second is triple-digit and refers to diameter. So a 28-622 tyre will only fit on a 622mm diameter rim, aka 700Cc, the most common road size.

How to tell what wheel size to get using your frame and fork

This one's a toughie – even seasoned mechanics find it hard – but there are ways to tell. If you can try on a wheel you

already have or borrow one from a friend, that's a fantastic place to start. But if you bought a frame without wheels, you'll need to do some sleuthing based on the frame type and age. If it's a vintage road frame, it'll probably have taken 27 x 1 ¼" or 700c wheels. If it's a British vintage cruiser frame, it might have taken 26 x 1 ⅜" or 26 x 1 ¼". If it's a French vintage frame, it may have taken 650B. Currently, the most common size for single-speed rear wheels is 700c. It's possible to get a custom-built rear single-speed wheel made in 27 x 1 ¼"

(ETRTO 630), 26 x 1 3/8" (ETRTO 590), and others – just ask your local bike shop. While these wheels are different sizes, frames can accommodate them within a certain range. Just make sure you have enough clearance (ie the tyre doesn't touch the frame/brakes). You may have to test different lengths of brake calipers though, to make sure the brake pads reach the rims. If you're really lost, take it to your LBS. They'll sort you out.

Selecting the right hubs

Once you have the right wheel size, you'll need to make sure that its hub is correct for your frame as well. Most modern front hubs will still fit older frames. The 100mm spacing on forks has been happily standardised for some time now. The two places you may run into a problem with a fork is if the dropouts are too narrow for the wheel axle, or the fork arms themselves are too narrow. If the fork is steel, you can use a file to slightly widen the dropouts (working really gently, checking often to make sure you don't go too far), and pry the arms apart to fit the hub. Don't do this if the fork isn't steel!

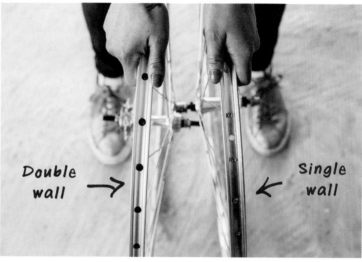

Double wall →

← Single wall

Rear single-speed and flip-flop hubs will have an over-locknut distance anywhere from 110 to 120mm. Over-locknut distance is the measurement from one locknut to the other (not to be confused with the wheelnut, which holds the wheel to the frame). Let's say your hub is 120mm – if your frame has an internal rear dropout measurement of 126mm (a common size on older bikes), and if the frame is steel, you can squeeze the frame to a narrower size as you tighten the wheelnuts. If the dropout spacing is wider than this, and your frame is steel,

you can cold set the frame. Cold setting means using physical force to move the frame into a desired position. This should be done by a pro though.

The quickest and easiest way to get your bike on the road will be to get a pair of 700c wheels, with the rear hub ready for either a single-speed freewheel or fixed/ freewheel combination (also known as a 'flip-flop' hub). A flip-flop hub will have threads on either side to accommodate a freewheel and a fixed sprocket/lockring. It is not possible to use a screw-on hub that is meant for gears.

TYRES, INNER TUBES AND RIMS

Choosing tyre diameter

Wheel size will dictate the diameter of tyre to get. If you have 700c wheels, you'll need 700c tyres, ERTRO 622.

Choosing tyre width

What width of tyre should you get? Go wide, baby, the widest you can! Your frame will dictate what width of tyre to get. You need clearance between the tyre and the following: fork crown, brake caliper, seat stays, chain stays, seat tube and any bridges between stays. I recommend 15mm clearance, bare minimum.

Wide tyres are way more comfortable to ride, they're more grippy, they have less rolling resistance, and they're just as fast as skinny tyres. If you're riding in the city, get the most puncture-proof tyres you can afford. And avoid knobbly tyres while in the city – they're great for off-road riding, but can reduce grip while riding on smooth road surfaces.

Tyre beads and wheel rims

Most modern tyres, save for the folding types, have a 'bead', a wire that runs along the inside of the tyre's edge. Modern rims are called

Check your tyre and mudguard clearance

'clincher' rims, and have a curved edge. The tyre's bead hooks under the rim's curved edge. Old wheels don't have this curved edge – the rims just go straight up and down. This means modern tyres don't have anything to hook on to on old wheels when you pump them up. If this is what you have, underinflate your tyres so that they don't go over the rims and explode. For example, if your tyres say 'inflate to 100psi', stop about 70psi if you don't have clincher rims.

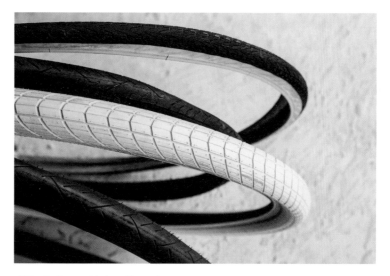

Double wall vs single wall rims

Do you want single-wall or double-wall rims? Single-walls are generally found on wider rims and can accommodate wider tyres at lower pressure. They tend to be cheaper too. Double-walls are found on narrower rims and take higher-pressure tyres. They are stronger than single wall, and more durable. I recommend getting doubles over singles.

Steel rims vs alloy rims

Vintage rims are often made of steel rather than alloy. Steel rims are durable, but inefficient for braking. They squeak in the rain, and modern brake pads have a difficult time gripping. If you have steel rims, get leather brake pads to make braking more efficient.

Choosing inner tubes

Inner tubes will fit a range of tyre sizes. If your tyre is 700 x 25, get a tube that's sized to fit 700 x 18 to 700 x 28. Depending on the valve hole in your rim, you'll need either a Schrader or Presta valve. Most narrow 700c and 27 x 1 ¼" rims will use a Presta valve, while wider rims will take a Schrader valve. They use different pump fixtures – usually found on opposing sides of the same pump head.

And finally... rim tape

If you have low-pressure tyres (below 80psi) and single-wall rims, you can get away with rubber rim tape. If you have double-wall rims, high-pressure tyres (above 80psi), or both, get cloth rim tape to protect the tube from punctures.

DRIVETRAIN

The drivetrain is the engine of your bike. It's literally what makes the wheels go round (that, and your legs, of course), so it's important to choose decent components to make sure it runs smoothly.

Bottom bracket

A square-taper, sealed cartridge bottom bracket is best. It's inexpensive, reliable and available in different spindle widths and cup threading to suit all sorts of bikes. Get the best your money can buy, as it's the heart of your bicycle.

The most common type is British thread, where the threading is reversed on the drive-side of the frame (righty loosey). Italian/French threads are regular thread on both sides – but this makes it prone to coming loose over time. Swiss threads are the same thread pitch as French threads but with a reverse thread on the drive-side like British threads. Tricksies.

Measure the width of the bottom bracket shell with your vernier calipers to determine if your frame is British thread or Italian thread (or possibly something else). If it's 68mm, it's British thread. Or possibly French (check the make of the frame).

If it's 70mm it's Italian, and if it's 71mm it's Raleigh/Carlton, a rare size, and one that can cause issues as conventional bottom brackets won't work with these bottom bracket shells.

Threadless bottom bracket

One way to get around damaged threads and unconventional threading issues is to get a threadless bottom bracket. This type of bottom bracket screws into itself, rather than the frame, so it gets around problem threads. It's not without its own problems (they tend to unscrew over time), but are a relatively inexpensive solution. Velo Orange makes a good one.

Chainline

Chainline is *very* important on a single-speed bike. Chainline means how parallel the chain is to the centre line of the bike frame. The chain runs from the chainring to the rear sprocket and back again – if it runs on too extreme a diagonal, it could make the chain come off while you're riding. It needs to be as straight as possible.

The bottom bracket spindle width will determine how close the

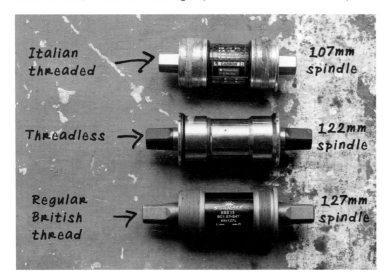

Italian threaded →   107mm spindle

Threadless →   122mm spindle

Regular British thread →   127mm spindle

chainset is to the frame, and by extension, the chainline.

So here's how to choose the correct spindle width. If your frame already has a bottom bracket and single-speed chainset, it's very likely you can keep the same width of bottom bracket. If you are replacing a double or triple chainset (two or three front chainrings), you will probably need a narrower bottom bracket. If your frame is from the '70s/'80s and has a rear dropout spacing of 126mm (or thereabouts), a good size to start with is 107-110mm bottom bracket spindle. Unfortunately there's no hard and fast way of calculating the perfect bottom bracket spindle length, so if this is too wide or narrow, you'll need to experiment with other sizes. This is where your local bike shop or community bike space comes in handy – they'll have different sizes of bottom brackets that you can test to get your chainline right. Keep in mind that a 110mm bottom bracket, while 3mm shorter than a 113mm bottom bracket, will only have 1.5mm of difference on either side.

This chain line is pretty good

Cotter pins in cottered cranks

How to tell if you can reuse your three-piece bottom bracket

Once you've taken your old three-piece bottom bracket out, clean it with a rag and inspect both the cups, and the cones of the spindle. If they have any pitting or uneven wear on the cups and cones, you should replace the three-piece bottom bracket with a square taper. (See p78 for an example of wear.) If they look smooth, you can go ahead and reuse the three-piece, so long as you replace all the bearings, and that the spindle length is compatible with a single-speed. If it came from a double or triple crankset, you probably won't be able to reuse this spindle, as it will be too long. If it came from a cottered crankset, I also recommend switching to a sealed square-taper bottom bracket.

Chainset

Or, in other words, the crank arms and chainring together. You will need a square-taper single-speed chainset to work with a square-taper bottom bracket. You have two options: an all-in-one chainset, where the crank arm is pressed on to the chainring, or one with a removable chainring that detaches from the crank arm. The all-in-one will probably be cheaper, but a removable chainring means that when the chainring wears out (and it *will* someday), you only have to replace the chainring itself, and not the entire chainset. I recommend the latter, as it also allows more flexibility with the chainring's tooth count, making it customisable, and it's stronger too. Note: if your chainring is $1/8$" or $3/32$" wide, you'll need to get a matching-width freewheel and chain.

Freewheel/fixed sprocket

Your single-speed rear hub will either have one side threaded, or both sides threaded.

The side with 'stepped' threads, where the outer portion is slightly narrower than the inner portion, is for a fixed-gear sprocket and lockring. If you look closely, you'll notice the threads are going in opposing directions. The side that just goes straight up and down is for a freewheel.

I recommend getting a single-speed freewheel to start out, rather than a fixed-gear sprocket, and that's what this book focuses on. A freewheel is a ratcheting sprocket (one that can turn independently of the wheel), which will make it more comfortable to ride. Fixed wheel basically means the pedals turn in time with the rear wheel – ie no coasting. This means you can't stop pedalling, whether you're going downhill, or over bumps.

They're great, but do require a different type of riding skill and awareness. It also helps for your feet to be attached to the pedal in some way, be it with cleats or toe straps. The good news is, it's pretty easy to convert a single-speed bike to a fixed gear, especially if you have a flip-flop hub. You don't need a rear brake either, for obvious reasons. However, that's as much detail as I'm going to go into in this book.

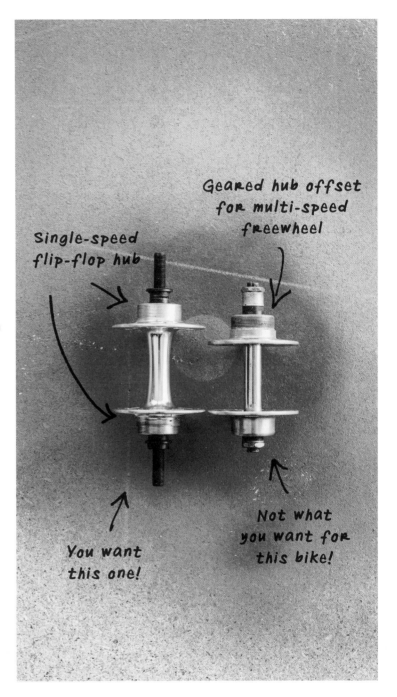

Geared hub offset for multi-speed freewheel

Single-speed flip-flop hub

You want this one!

Not what you want for this bike!

Gear ratios – how many teeth should you get?

One reason bicycles are such efficient forms of transport is because of gear ratios. Different numbers of teeth on the chainring and rear sprocket allow a rider to go faster and further using minimal effort. A large number of teeth in the front and a small number of teeth in the back (for example: 52t x 16t) will mean a hard gearing, great for going fast. Conversely, a small number in the front and large number in the back (46t x 22t) will mean easy gearing, suited for gentle pedalling or hills.

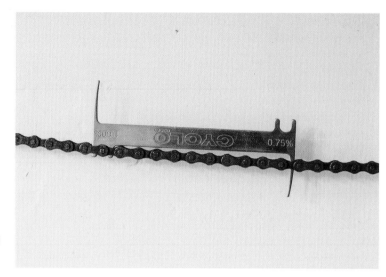

It's important to start out with a gear ratio that will allow you to ride comfortably in the environment you plan on using this bike. One easy way to work this out is if you have a bike already – think about which front and rear sprockets you use the most, then count the number of teeth on each. You can then choose a chainset and freewheel with the same number of teeth. But chainsets and freewheels are only made with certain numbers of teeth – what if your numbers aren't covered? Easy – figure out the ratio of front teeth to back teeth, then obtain a chainset and rear sprocket of the same ratio. For example, if you like riding in a 50t x 25t combination, your ratio is 2:1. You could get a 44t front chainset with a 22t rear freewheel to reflect the same ratio.

But if you've not got a bike to do this, or you'll be using your bike in unfamiliar terrain, here are some example starter ratios for different environments. Note that it's best to start out with an easier gearing, as a harder one could wreak havoc on your knees.

A Commuting on flat roads: 2.3:1
B MTB cross-country: 1.75:1
C Hilly roads: 2:1

There are websites, apps and forums dedicated to the study of gear ratios, gear inches, gain inches and numerous offshoots.

Chain

After you've chosen a chainset and sprocket, you'll need the correctly sized chain. If you are reusing your old chain, use a chain wear indicator to check if it can be reused. Its indicators measure how much the bushings on the chain have worn down. There are usually two numbers on each side: .75% and 1%. Drop the indicator into the chain, as above, and see what it corresponds with: 75% means you need to replace the chain, and 1% means you must replace the chain and freewheel. See p36 for more detail on this.

Chains come in different widths that are based on the number of gears on your bike. So in our case, for a single-speed bike, we'll need a single-speed chain. Chains are the canary in the coal mine – they wear down the quickest out of your drivetrain components, and should be checked every few months. Purchase the best chain your money can buy, as this usually means it will last longer. And make sure it comes with a quick link.

A note on chain width

There are two widths of
single-speed chain and
single-speed components
(chainring and rear sprocket)
out there: $3/32$" and $1/8$".
The first is more commonly
found on town bikes and
is slightly narrower. The
second is commonly found
on track bikes, and is ever
so slightly wider. Both are
considered single-speed
widths. You *can* use a $1/8$"
chain on $3/32$" components,
but you risk them making
a clickety sound as you
ride. A $3/32$" chain will not
fit on $1/8$" components.
So be sure that you choose
the correct chain width
for the components that
you obtain.

HEADSET, HANDLEBARS AND STEM

If your frame came with a headset already, check to see if it's worth keeping. Definitely replace the bearings if they're loose. Ball bearings come in an assortment of sizes, so count how many you have in each cup, then take one to your local bike shop so that they can get you the correct size in the correct amount (get a couple of spare ones too). If the races have pitting, it's best to replace the whole thing. Headsets tend to fit together in a specific way, so replacing only one part could pose fitting issues.

If you're getting a new headset, measure the stack height to make sure it's the same as your old one (see p85). You will need to get a 1" threaded headset. I recommend one with sealed bearings (as opposed to loose bearings or a bearing cage), as they last longer and are easier to put together.

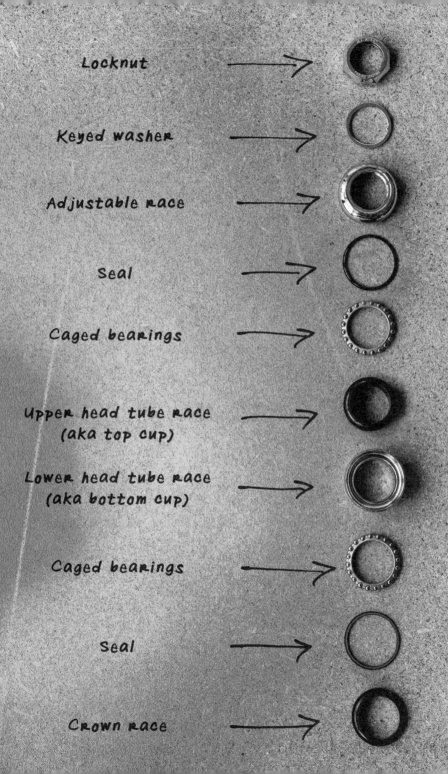

Locknut →

Keyed washer →

Adjustable race →

Seal →

Caged bearings →

Upper head tube race
(aka top cup) →

Lower head tube race
(aka bottom cup) →

Caged bearings →

Seal →

Crown race →

Stem

For a threaded 1" headset, you'll need a quill stem. These can come in different heights, lengths and angles.

Choose one that's suitable for the type of riding you'll be doing. For a more upright riding position, get a stem that'll give a lot of height, a slightly shorter reach length and an upward angle. For a more racy riding position, choose a shorter height, a longer reach and a downward angle.

The diameter of the stem clamp will need to match the diameter of the centre of the handlebars. The standard clamp size is 25.4mm, but there are other variations so be sure to measure.

Handlebars

This is a bit like choosing what kind of hairstyle you'll have for your bike. Different bars are great for different types of 'ride feel', so be sure to choose one that suits the type of cycling you'll be doing. Just make sure that the diameter of your handlebar matches the diameter of your stem clamp.

Drop bars are great for road riding and longer rides, as the drop shape allows for three different riding positions. Straight bars or riser bars give more control, and the wider you go, the more comfortable the ride. Swept-back bars are ideal for commuting, leisure and city riding. They're very comfortable and allow for greater visibility while riding.

There's a whole world of handlebars out there, and these are just a few variations.

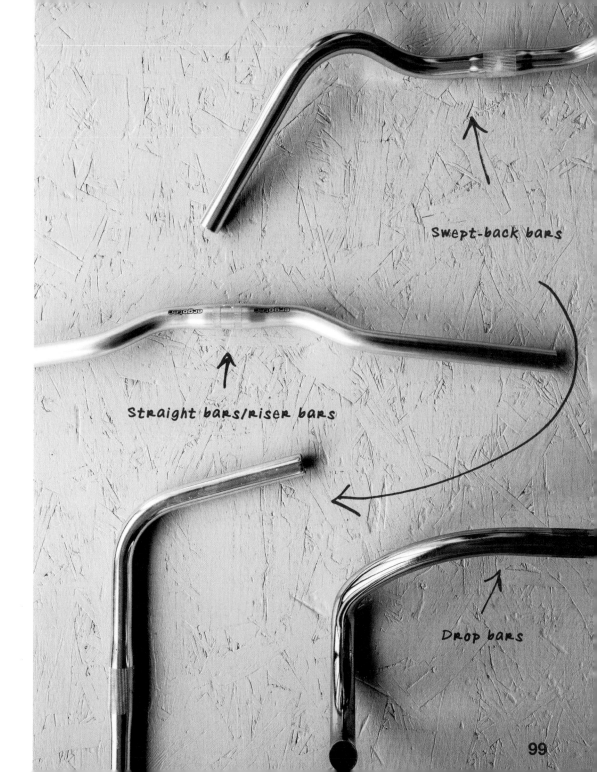

Swept-back bars

Straight bars/riser bars

Drop bars

BRAKES

Your frame, handlebars and wheels will dictate what type of brakes you should get. For this book, I'll be showing you how to choose the correct caliper rim brake for your bike, but there are other options out there, like disc, hub, cantilever and V-brakes.

Choosing brake arm length
Firstly, put the front wheel in the fork, and measure the distance between the centre of the brake hole on the fork to the centre of the rim. Do this on the rear too. This will help you choose caliper brakes with the correct reach. They come in three lengths:

Short reach: 39-49mm
Normal reach: 47-57mm
Long reach: 55-73mm

Short-reach calipers are more efficient at braking than long, so if your measurement falls between two reaches, go for the shorter version. If you're able to test different lengths, attach the brake and squeeze the arms against the rim (making sure the pads are in the right place) and see where the pads touch. If they touch the tyre and can't go down further,

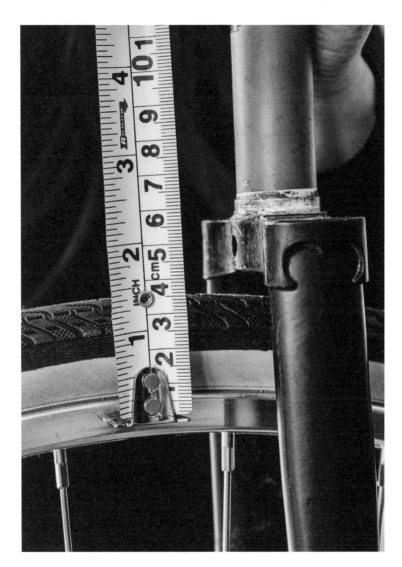

the arms are too short. If they are coming off the bottom of the rim, and can't come up any further, the arms are too long.

Recessed nut vs standard nut

Your frame and fork will also determine if you should get a modern recessed nut or vintage standard nut on the front and rear brakes. New standard nutted brakes are available but usually only in long-reach versions. These are made to accommodate 700c wheels in 27 x 1 ¼" frames/forks.

If you have a vintage frameset with 6mm holes, you'll need nutted brakes. If your frameset is drilled to take an 8mm recessed nut you can get modern brakes. Note: front brake bolts are longer than rear ones. It's possible to drill out the back of your fork from 6mm up to 8mm to accommodate a recessed nut – a more advanced bike-building technique, so go slowly!

If the recessed nut won't fit on the rear brake bridge, you might be able to use a modern front brake (which will have a longer bolt). Just make sure you have the appropriate curved washers if the bridge is a tube. This will help secure it. Drilling the bridge isn't a great idea, and can be hard because the seat tube is in the way.

Nutted front brake

Recessed-nut front brake

Brake levers

Handlebars will dictate what brake levers you need. If you have drop bars, their diameter is probably 23.8mm and you have the choice of two levers: drop (which themselves come in two styles: aero and non-aero), and cross-top. If you have flat, swept-back or riser bars, their measurement is probably 22.2mm and you can use cross-top, flat-bar or bar-end levers. All require matching the diameter of the clamp to your bars. Bar-end levers go *into* the ends of the bars so need to match the *internal diameter* of the bars, usually 19-22mm for 23.8-26mm diameter drop bars, although Dia-Compe makes a pair to fit 22.2mm bars with a narrower 16-19mm internal diameter.

Brake cables

The brake cable you need will depend on the brake levers you have. If you have road brake levers, you'll likely need road brake cables, aka pear-end brake cables. If you have flat-bar levers, you might need mountain bike brake cables, also known as barrel-end brake cables – but just as likely you might need road brake cables. Have a look at the place where the cable end will be fitted in the lever. If it's shaped like a cup, you'll need a pear-end cable. If it's a separate cage with a circular cutaway for the cable end, it's for a barrel-end cable.

You'll also need brake housing, which makes the brakes work. Brake housing is 5mm in diameter and made of a plastic inner tube, a coiled helix of wire and a plastic outer. Your frame will dictate how much you need, but get at least 2m to be safe. And don't forget ferrules and cable end caps.

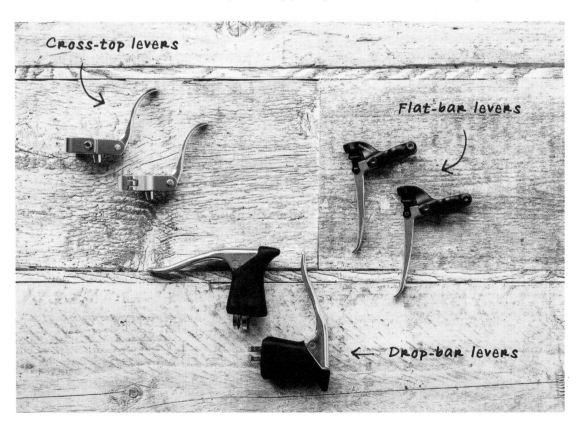

Cross-top levers

Flat-bar levers

Drop-bar levers

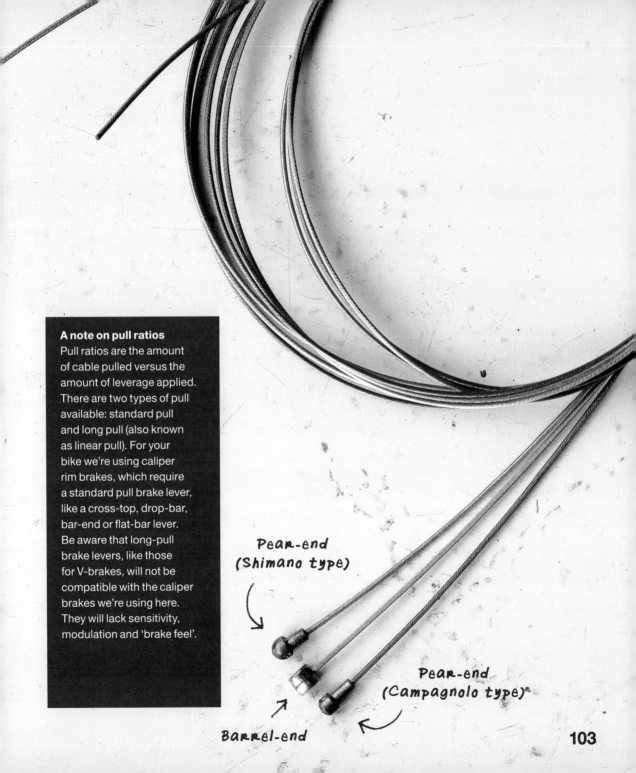

A note on pull ratios

Pull ratios are the amount of cable pulled versus the amount of leverage applied. There are two types of pull available: standard pull and long pull (also known as linear pull). For your bike we're using caliper rim brakes, which require a standard pull brake lever, like a cross-top, drop-bar, bar-end or flat-bar lever. Be aware that long-pull brake levers, like those for V-brakes, will not be compatible with the caliper brakes we're using here. They will lack sensitivity, modulation and 'brake feel'.

Pear-end
(Shimano type)

Pear-end
(Campagnolo type)

Barrel-end

SEATPOST, SADDLE AND PEDALS

If there was a seatpost on your frame when you got it, wonderful. If there wasn't, you will need to be extra-precise in choosing a seatpost, as they come in increments of .2mm. A 25.4mm seatpost will not fit in a frame that requires 25.6mm. Some older frames, like vintage Peugeots, have very rare small-sized seatposts. In this instance you will have to turn to eBay, bike jumbles, a local bike shop or an online retailer that specialises in vintage bikes.

Use a pair of vernier calipers to measure the inside diameter of your seat tube. If you're getting different readings from different positions, use the average.

Saddle

The saddle will depend on your riding position and the width of your sit bones. Women are quick to think they have wide sit bones, and so need a big padded saddle, but this is not necessarily the case – skinny guys can have wide sit bones too! This means that it's a very personal experience. Your bum is the part of your body that demands comfort more than any other, and on longer rides you'll really notice if the saddle isn't right. If you want to ride in a racy position, choose a racing saddle. These tend to be narrow to allow your body to be in a crouched position. Some saddles have cutaways to relieve perineal pressure.

If you're riding in a relaxed position, you'll need a wider saddle, as much of your body weight will be on your sit bones. And if your position is somewhere in between, seek out a 'touring' saddle, one that will allow for different riding positions. Big, wide padded saddles are not the most comfortable – in fact, some of the best saddles around are hard ones that prop up your body. It all depends on your riding position and body shape.

Due to its sensitive nature, the saddle often is the part of the bike that gets changed the most, so you might not want to splurge straight away. Take your time – get your sit bones expertly measured at a specialist bike shop or with a professional bike fitter, and see if they have test saddles you can borrow.

Pedals

Pedals are an oft overlooked part of a bike – they're just flat spinny bits, right? But the correct pedal can make your ride that much more comfortable. Vintage road pedals tended to have toe clips, and so they are weighted for the top of the pedal to be flipped down in its resting state. This allows the rider to easily slip their foot into the toe clip as they flip the pedal up. However, without the toe clip, weighted pedals are massively annoying to ride because the other side of the pedal isn't flat at all.

If you don't want to use toe clips, proper flat pedals are the way to go. There are hundreds of styles and colours: yet another chance to personalise your ride. Make sure you get $^9/_{16}$" sized pedals to fit your cranks ($½$" pedals are for children's bikes), and note that French threading also exists on vintage French pedals/cranks.

If you're interested in longer rides, using 'clipless pedals' will help with more efficient power transfer. This is a system where cleats on the sole of special shoes can be clipped in to the pedal, so you can pull as well as push when you ride: great for attacking hills. I recommend starting with Shimano SPDs, practising in a park riding with cleats, and repeating to yourself: 'Clip out, clip out, clip out…' Also, if you're riding a fixed-gear bicycle, you really need some sort of foot/pedal retention, in the form of clipless pedals or toe straps.

Pedals are 'sided', as one is meant for the right side of the bike and the other is meant for the left. You should be able to see the letters 'R' and 'L' on the end of the axle and if you look closely you can see the threads actually go in opposing directions. They are another part of the bike where there is a reverse thread, this time on the non-drive-side. Pedals tighten going towards the front of the bike and loosen going back.

PUTTING IT ALL TOGETHER

So now we move on to the most exciting bit of the book. How to build your very own bicycle. You've put the planning in, you've got the parts, you're ready to go. Remember to eat breakfast before you start, take breaks when you need them, and brew a cuppa if you get a bit befuddled. If you struggle at any point, no worries - it's all part of the process. Remember, nothing worth it was ever easy. Are you ready to get your hands dirty? Let's get building!

01

Mount the frame

- I recommend using a workstand to put everything together: it just makes it all easier. Start by putting your frame securely in. If it's freshly painted, put a clean rag in the clamp and don't overtighten, or put the seatpost and seatpost bolt/collar in at this point and clamp the seatpost.
- You want the drive-side of the bike facing you. A wise mechanic once told me it's bad luck to do otherwise. (I think she was joking, but just to be sure…)

02

Insert the bottom bracket

- First, thoroughly coat the threads of the bottom bracket shell with anti-seize or grease (see p24). Don't be shy. I'm talking an obscene amount of grease. Sacrilegious even. So much you can't see the threads. You can never have too much grease. (You can, however, have too much oil.)
- You should know the type of threading you have in your frame by now. Remember which direction to tighten? No? Go back to p66 and revise.

Three-piece bottom bracket

Gather these tools:

_ Lockring spanner
_ Adjustable cup tool
_ Fixed cup tool

• If you're reusing your old three-piece bottom bracket (or putting in a new one), start by putting a nice bed of grease in the fixed cup. Don't skimp!

• Then, using your fingers or a long narrow tool that's magnetised (like a screwdriver), carefully place new correctly sized ball bearings around the cup like a pearl necklace.

• Fill it completely with bearings, then take one out – you want a small gap in between the bearings, they shouldn't be bunched up against each other.

• Put more grease over the top of all the bearings.

• Do the same with the adjustable cup (the non-drive-side bearing cup).

• Insert the fixed cup on the drive-side and turn in the appropriate direction. If it's British thread, turn counterclockwise. If it's Italian or French thread, turn clockwise.

• Tighten shoulder tight with the appropriate tool.

- The spindle *may* be equidistant from the centre, but it's possible that one side will be longer than the other. This is to accommodate the chainring taking up space on the drive-side. If one side is longer, that end will be put in first. If they're both the same size, either side can go in first. Enter from the non-drive-side of the bottom bracket shell, placing it into the hole in the fixed cup until it stops. The cone on the spindle will be butting up against the bearings.

- Now screw on the adjustable cup. Adjust the tightness of the cup on the non-drive-side to create a spindle that spins freely, but doesn't have any play. Keep testing the spindle for play (too loose) and grinding (too tight) when tightening or loosening the adjustable cup to find the sweet spot, like Goldilocks. When using old components there's a chance you'll have to compromise. In this instance, better to have a bit of play rather than any grinding.

- The final step is to screw on the lockring with a lockring spanner. This will keep the adjustable cup in the proper position.

Sealed cartridge bottom bracket

Gather this tool:

__ Cartridge bottom bracket tool

• If you're using a square-taper cartridge bottom bracket, insert the large sealed portion of the bottom bracket into the drive-side and turn in the appropriate direction by hand – don't use a tool yet. The cup should turn smoothly and without much resistance. If you feel like you need to force it at this point, stop and back off. You could be going in at an angle and cross-threading the frame, damaging it in the process.

• Once the threads have caught, you can screw in the non-drive-side retaining cup halfway. This will help guide the bottom bracket in straight.

• Go back to the drive-side and use the cartridge bottom bracket tool to ensure the cup is fully screwed into the frame, and shoulder tighten.

• Once the drive-side of the bottom bracket is fully in place, you can screw in the non-drive-side cup. This side isn't as important to get completely in; it's more there to make sure that the bottom

bracket is held in the centre of the bottom bracket shell. It may even be the case that if you tighten it too much, the pressure won't allow the bottom bracket to spin easily, so test the spindle once you're done tightening to make sure it hasn't been affected.

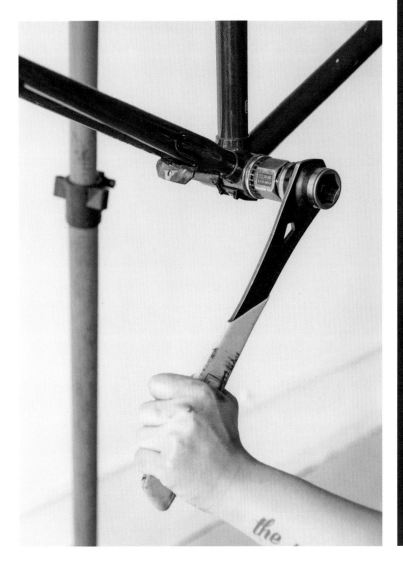

Troubleshooting

• Always make sure you clean bottom bracket threads beforehand with a good bike frame cleaner and steel wool – but sometimes threads can be worn and *caked* with dirt. To DIY clean, you can use an old (but clean) steel BB cup with the correct thread pitch for the correct side of the shell. Slowly tighten the threads of the bottom bracket one turn, then back off a half turn, and then tighten again for one turn, and backing off a half turn again. Repeat this process to help get the gunk out of the threads.

• Make sure the threads on the BB cup are the appropriate pitch for your frame. If the cup seems to tighten for a couple of turns but then immediately stops, it could be that the thread pitches don't match.

• Sometimes there's a gear cable guide on the underside of the bottom bracket shell, and there could be a little plastic nub or screw that sticks out inside the bottom bracket shell. This could prevent a sealed bottom bracket from making it all the way through. Get rid of it! We're making a single-speed bike, so there's no need for a gear cable guide.

03

Attach the chainset

- Slide the drive-side crank arm on to the bottom bracket spindle, and tighten the crank bolt with the appropriate tool. Make sure you have purchase here – you don't want the tool slipping and rounding out the bolt. Shoulder tighten: you want these cranks to stay on!
- Slide the left-side crank arm on to the bottom bracket spindle, making sure it's opposite the right-side arm.
- Tighten the crank bolt shoulder-tight.

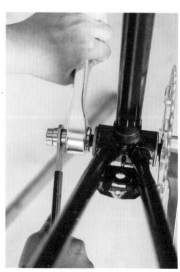

04

Attach the pedals

- Put a small amount of anti-seize or grease on the threads of the crank arm.
- Make sure you're using the correct pedal for each side of the bike. Pedals are often labelled 'R' or 'L' on the end of the axle. Now, this is very important to remember – the left-hand pedal is reverse threaded. So on the left side of your bike, you'll be turning anticlockwise to tighten. The right-hand pedal is regular thread. Another way to remember this is that pedals tighten going in the forward direction of your bike, and loosen going back. I have seen too many people destroy their cranks because they didn't know that pedals are 'sided' – be very careful!
- Pedals tighten as you ride, so there's no need to tighten them like The Hulk would.

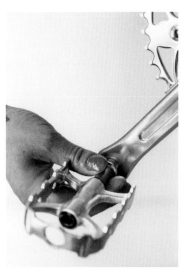

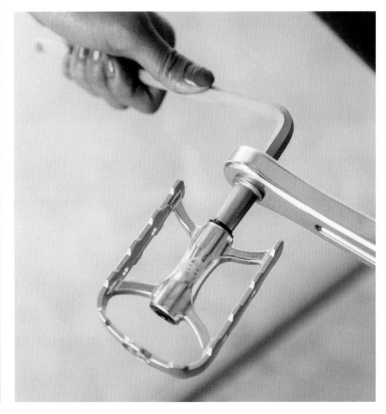

Attach the headset
- The 1" threaded headset will be made up of the following parts, from the bottom up: crown race (which attaches to the forks), bearings, bottom cup (aka lower head-tube race), top cup (aka upper head-tube race), bearings, adjustable race and locknut (see p97 for a diagram).
- Remove any bearings, whether sealed or loose, from the cups.

Crown race

- Let's start with the crown race. If you happen to have a split crown race, lucky you! Just slide that baby on and be done with it. But if you have a complete ring, use the crown race setter.

- Put a nice ring of grease around the protruding edge of the fork steerer tube, just above the fork crown – the point where the crown race will be making contact. (As we all know, lube allows for easier insertion.)

- Place the crown race on top of this edge. Make sure the flat side is facing down. The crown race setter is like a circular hammer – you're going to gently bang this baby on to the fork crown.

- Hold the fork in one hand, raise the crown race setter towards the top end of the tube, and bring it down hard on to the crown race. Be firm, and be even. It will probably take several whacks before it settles nicely down on to the fork crown. Don't place the fork on a solid surface – you could damage the fork blades while hammering.

- If the crown race just doesn't go on, it's probably because it's JIS (Japanese Industrial Standard) sized. See p123 to find out what you can do about it.

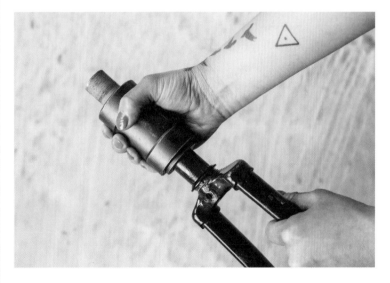

Headset cups

• Take your time and pay attention! Get yourself familiar with the headset press too. No matter which kind you are using, they all do the same thing: press headset cups (the lower and upper head tube races) into your frame. I like to do both mine at the same time, but your tool may only let you do one at a time.

• Apply anti-sieze or grease to the inside edge of the top and bottom of the head tube, where the cups make contact with the frame.

• Place the appropriate cup in position – top cup on top, bottom cup on bottom.

• Align any writing on the cups in the position you'd like them to be.

• Take the headset press and remove one end and the stepped ring (if there is one).

• Slide the press into the top of the headset tube and align the stepped ring on the top cup.

• Place the second stepped ring on the bottom so that it's up against the bottom cup, and reattach the other end of the headset press until it clicks into place.

- Turn the handles until the stepped ring is gently holding the bottom cup in place. Take a second to make sure your cups are straight here and still in proper alignment.
- Now start turning the handles in a clockwise direction, holding the axle still with your other hand. This will bring the cups in towards each other, pressing them into the frame. Progress slowly, checking that they're still in alignment. If they're a tiny bit crooked, like a 1mm difference, that's OK – but 2mm or more difference means you should stop and re-straighten. If the cup doesn't budge, take the headset press out, and use the headcup remover to tap the cup out (see p59), and start over again.
- Keep turning the handles until the cups are fully in the frame. One may go in first, before the other – this is fine, just keep going until the other cup goes in too.
- Wipe off any grease that may have come out the sides.
- Inspect the head tube at the point where the cup and head tube are making contact – you don't want to see any light shining through the gaps.

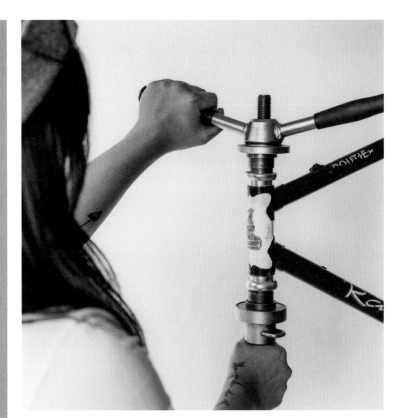

Bearings

You'll either have loose bearings, caged bearings or sealed bearings. If your headset is secondhand I highly recommend putting in new bearings. In fact, I insist on it. There could be tiny dents or fractures that the eye can't catch, and these will get worse over time. Putting in new bearings gives a headset a new lease of life.

Loose bearings (as in 'Three-piece bottom bracket', p110)

- Put a nice bed of grease around the inside of the cup.
- Individually place enough bearings to fill up the entire ring, then take one out.
- Put even more grease on top of the bearings. This acts like glue and will prevent them from falling out before you put in the fork.

Caged bearings

- Easy peasy – just make sure you're putting them in the right way round!
- Put a nice bed of grease around the inside of the cup. On the bottom cup you'll want the flat side of the cage facing up so that the bearings are making contact with the crown race.
- Put even more grease on top of the bearings. Similarly, on the top cup you'll want the flat side of the cage facing up. The bearings need to make contact with the upper head tube race. If you put it in the wrong way round, the headset is gonna feel grindy.
- Make sure you put a ton of grease on the bottom and top of the bearings – be generous. If the cages are damaged, you can replace them with loose ball bearings and follow the previous instructions.

Sealed bearings

- Just make sure you're replacing like for like. You can get replacement bearings from the manufacturer of your headset, or your local bike shop. Sealed bearings are great – just pop them in and they're ready to go.
- Make sure the bevelled edge is aligned with the edge of the crown race and the top cup.
- No need to grease them, there's grease already inside.

Insert the threaded fork

• Carefully place the fork steerer tube through the head tube, and screw on the top adjustable race so that it's flush with the top headset cup. If you have loose or caged bearings, now is the time for the Goldilocks technique – you have to find the sweet spot where the bearings aren't too tight or too loose, but *juuuust* right. To test this, grab a fork arm with one hand and the head tube with the other. See if you can wiggle the fork steerer tube from side to side inside the head tube. If it feels like there's some wiggle room, or some 'knocking', it's too loose.

Tighten the adjustable race slightly and test again. Swivel the fork around. If it feels stiff or 'grindy', it's too tight. Continue to tighten or loosen to find the spot where there's no knocking, but no grinding either.

• When you find it, add the keyed washer (if there is one), then screw on the locknut. Use two headset spanners or an adjustable spanner to tighten the locknut against the adjustable race. Hold the adjustable race still with one hand, while you tighten the locknut with the other hand. Test again after tightening for the sweet spot and adjust if necessary.

• The beauty of sealed bearings is that you don't need to do this back-and-forth. Simply tighten the adjustable race hand-tight, make sure there's no play, add the keyed washer, if there is one, then screw on the locknut. Hold the adjustable race still while you tighten the locknut against it.

JIS vs ISO standardisation

Depending on the age of your bike, you may have a 27mm fork crown, which is an old Japanese Industrial Standard (JIS) size, rather than the currently more common International Standards Organisation (ISO) size of 26.6mm. You have a couple of options here. One is to get a JIS-specific headset. Or you could take the fork into your local bike shop to get the fork crown milled down to the correct diameter. Your DIY solution here is to file down the ring, little by little, testing along the way with the crown race setter to make sure you haven't gone to far! You do not want this ring to become too small, as a loose crown race will mean that your headset is going to be loose and unstable, easily causing damage to your headset and potentially your head tube.

07

Attach the freewheel

- Put a small amount of anti-seize or grease on the threads of the freewheel side of the wheel hub. (Make sure it's not the stepped side, which is for fixed sprockets.)
- Using your hand, carefully screw on the freewheel, making sure it's going on straight and you're not forcing it. If it doesn't go, you may be cross-threading, so stop! Hopefully you can then just use your fingers in the splines of the freewheel to unscrew it. If not, you'll need a freewheel removal tool that matches the shape of your freewheel, or a hammer and punch to tap and unscrew the freewheel.
- Once the freewheel is on, you can do a final tighten with a freewheel tool, but the chain will tighten it as as you ride, so no need to do it loads.

Apply the rim tape

- Start by cutting a hole for the valve to pop through: to do this, fold about 2cm of the end of the rim tape on itself.
- Cut a triangle into the edge, but don't cut all the way to the side edges – leave 1-2mm. When you unfold the tape, you'll have a diamond shape that will allow the valve to go through.
- Place the diamond over the valve hole. Press the sticky side of the tape all the way round the rim.
- When you get back to the valve hole, cut the tape to a neat finish.

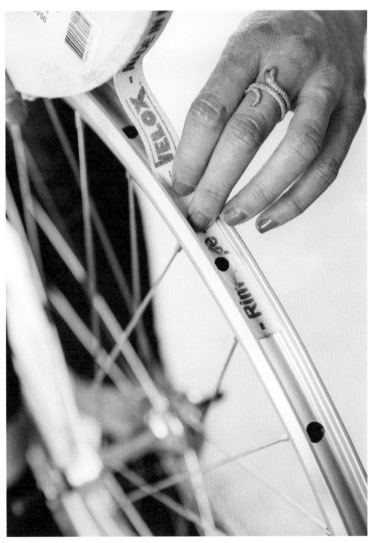

Put the tyres on the wheels

- Pump a bit of air inside the inner tube so that it takes a shape. This will make it quicker to put inside your tyre and avoid twisting (which can cause a pinch flat).
- Start by placing the valve inside the tyre where the label is. (This will make it easier to find punctures in the future – if you can find the culprit on your tyre, it'll be easier to find it on the inner tube.) Tuck the inner tube all the way around the tyre, taking care not to twist the tube.
- Place the wheel next to the tyre and line the valve up with the valve hole. Remove the screwed-on valve ring from the valve if you haven't already. As you put the valve inside the hole, notice that one side of the tyre already wants to start going in the rim of the wheel. The tyre rim that is touching the wheel rim will be the one that you start tucking inside first. Do not tuck in the other side! It will be impossible to get in both rims at the same time. Once you get one rim inside the wheel, go back to the

valve area and start tucking inside the other side of the tyre into the wheel rim. Use your thumbs to push the crossover points of where the tyre is going into the rim. Do not put on the valve ring at this stage – you'll do that only at the very end.

- Once it's all in, you're not done yet! First you need to check and make sure that no inner tube is stuck between the tyre and the rim. Start from the valve and go around the entire tyre, checking between the tyre and rim on both sides. If you see any inner tube, you have to take the tyre off one side and tuck the tube in all over again.
- Last step is to make sure the valve can move freely

in and out of the valve hole. Push the valve into the tyre. If it can go in and out easily, good. If it doesn't move, you need to force the valve in. If you pump it up and the valve is stuck under the tyre, it will explode and you'll need a new tube.

- Pump up your tyre to the correct PSI (pounds per square inch, an imperial unit of pressure). This is listed on the side of the tyre. It'll say something like 'Minimum pressure 30PSI – maximum pressure 80PSI'. There are variations, and it's good to know what your tyres require. I tend to pump my tyres up to the maximum pressure while riding in the city.

Tyre tips!
Putting it on may get tough towards the end…

- Deflate the inner tube completely.
- Starting across from the 'problem area', grab the wheel in one hand and tyre in the other. As you pull the wheel back, push the tyre towards the part that won't go in, bit by bit, to get slack where the tight spot is.
- As you do this, also pinch the tyre so that the tyre rim is in the centre of the wheel rim, and not on the stepped bit of the wheel rim. Sometimes tyres can get stuck on this ledge.
- Use the palms of your hands to alternatively roll each side of the crossover points of where the tyre is going into the rim.
- If it's really tight, you can try a bit of washing-up liquid to help slide the tyre in.
- Worst case scenario, you can use tyre levers, but you're taking the risk of getting a pinch flat.

10

Attach the wheels to the frame

• Now put both wheels in the frame, and tighten the locknuts or the quick-release skewers.

• Fork dropouts may be small on vintage forks, and you may need to file these with a metal file to fit a modern front wheel. This is normal, but proceed slowly as you don't want to file off too much. It's all beginning to look like something you could actually ride now – you know… a bike?

Attach the chain

Here's how to size your chain for length. A new chain is almost certainly going to be too long for your drivetrain – that's the way they're made and you'll need to trim it down.

Setting up

• Move the rear wheel as far forward in the dropouts as it can go, without coming out, and tighten the nuts. Make sure the wheel is straight and centred between the seat stays and chain stays. This is to ensure you have room to pull the wheel back to get the correct chain tension.

• Place the chain over the top of the front chainring and the rear freewheel, making sure you're going through the rear triangle of your frame.

• Wrap it round and bring the ends of the chain together at the bottom of the drivetrain. Note that the chain is made up of inner and outer links. You're going to use the quick link supplied with the chain to connect both ends of the chain, and it is going to take the place of one of the outer links.

• Pulling both ends of the chain together, pinpoint where an outer link connects with an inner link and creates a chain tension that's not too tight. A *bit* loose is OK, as you can pull the rear wheel back to tighten.

• Using the chain tool, remove the pin that exposes an inner link and removes an outer link, as the quick link needs two inner links to connect.

Connect the chain

Take the chain off the chainring to give yourself some slack – just make sure that the chain is definitely going through the rear triangle of the frame, and that it's not twisted. (See p52 for pictures of different quick links.)

Two-piece quick link

• Place one pin in one end of the chain, and the other pin in the other end, joining the chain together.
• Place the outer plate on one of the pins, then bend the rear plate inwards, so that the pins point towards each other – then push the outer plate on to the other pin.

Three-piece quick link

• Place one pin in one end of the chain, and the other pin in the other end of the chain, joining the chain together.
• Place the outer plate over both pins, and then place the larger gap of the outer spring clip over one of the pins.
• Then, using your hands or a pair of pliers, push the clip forward so that it clips on to both of the pins.

Shimano two-piece quick link

• Place one pin in one end of the chain and the other pin

in the other end of the chain, joining the chain together. Make sure the recessed side of the outer plate is facing out, and place the circular notch over one of the pins.

- Then slide the plate to the other end, so that the pin is now at the other end of the outer plate.
- Line up the circular notch over the other pin, bend the back plate two pins toward each other, and pop the outer plate on the other pin.
- If you have don't have a quick link, you'll be pushing through the pin to connect the inner and outer link. Back off the chain tool pin quite far as you need to make room for the whole pin.
- Push the inner link into the outer link and place the empty bushing between the teeth of the chain tool.
- Line up the pin with the chain tool's pin, and then turn the handle of the chain tool so that the pins line up. Now proceed slowly, making sure the chain pin is straight. Time to channel The Force – use your feelings and your eye, and stop turning when the back end of the pin is fully in and looks like the other pins of the chain.
- But what if it turns out your chain is just too short or too long when you try to size

it, like it's 'between' links? You'll need to get what's called a half link, the hobbit of the chain world. Half links are exactly that – half of a link. Complete half link chains are popular on BMXs but not so much on road bikes, as they weigh a lot more. In this instance though they're incredibly useful. Use one to extend your chain just enough so that the wheel is secure in the dropouts and there's still a bit of room to

pull back the wheel in the future (chains 'stretch' and lose tension over time). KMC makes a specific half link connector, or you can try getting one from a BMX-specific bike shop.

12

Tension the chain

• Chain tension can be hard to get right, and will probably be easier to do with your bike upside down. Tension is important as that's what ensures the chain stays on while you ride. Too loose and the chain will come off. Too tight and you won't be able to pedal, or your drivetrain will make a weird clacking sound. The chain shouldn't look baggy or slack, nor should it be completely rigid and stiff.

• Loosen the wheelnuts, pull the wheel back, and make sure the wheel is centred and the chain is tight. The chain should have about 5mm of movement both up and down.

• Turn the pedals and test for tighter and looser spots along the whole chain.

• Set the cranks in one of the tighter spots. Tighten the wheelnuts a little at a time on each side, making sure the

wheel is still straight and the tension is still good.

- Still need help getting the right chain tension? If you have a friend nearby, get them to push the wheel into the correct place, making sure it's straight in between the stays.
- If you don't have a spare pair of hands around, try a pair of tyre levers, one on each side of your tyre, in between the tyre and stay, to hold the wheel in the correct place.
- If you have a new chain, it'll already have a light lube on it, so there's no need to oil it at this time. When you start hearing tiny squeaks, that's when you should oil it. See p163 for more on maintenance.

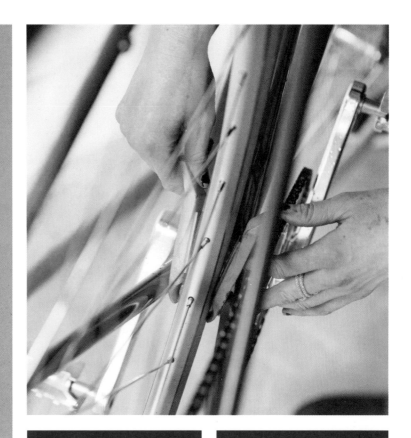

Top trick
Here's a BMX trick to getting your wheel straight. It's called 'walking the wheel', where you move the wheel side to side and back bit by bit, eventually getting the correct chain tension and a centred wheel. Start with the wheel in the frame with the nuts tight but not mega tight. Undo the nut on the drive-side and pull the axle as far as you can towards the back of the bike. The tyre will be touching the chainstay. This is OK. Tighten the nut.

Then undo the non-drive-side nut and pull the axle back until the wheel is better centred. The wheel may be crooked still; the chain may be slack, or too tight. This is OK. Tighten this nut. Then go back to your drive-side and loosen the nut. Pull back to tighten the chain/straighten the wheel – catch my drift? Repeat this process until you get the wheel centred and chain tensioned.

Insert the stem

• Start by applying some anti-seize or grease to the inside of the head tube where the stem will be making contact. Then put the stem into the tube.

• The height will be up to you but you must make sure that the minimum insertion point (marked on the stem) is below the headset locknut. If not enough of the stem is held securely in the frame, the stem could lever itself loose, causing damage to the head tube and headset, or even bend.

• Once it's in position, use the correctly sized hex key to tighten the stem bolt, first with the long end of the hex key, and then a final tighten with the short end – shoulder-tight.

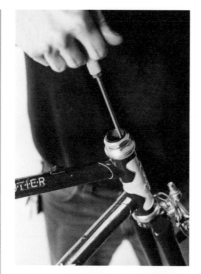

Attach the handlebars

- Most bars are straightforward to put in, but you'll need to make sure that the diameter matches up with your stem. Putting in a shim (a sort of metal sleeve to reduce the diamter) here is possible, but not ideal. Shims can slip. Get the right-sized bar for your stem.

- With drop bars, because there's a curve in the bar, it can be a bit fiddly to get them in. Start by making sure you're putting in the bars the right way forward. Insert the left end of the bar into the right side of the stem. Notice that the stem clamp has a wider and narrower point. When you get to the curve in your bar, turn the bars so that the inside of the curve is at the narrow point of the stem. This will allow you to tightly turn the bars to get around the curve.

- Once they're in position, check their angle. There's always room for adjustment later, but a good place to start for drop bars is to have the bottom of the drops parallel with the ground (see the picture on p139).

15

Attach the brake calipers

- Note the difference between the front and rear brake calipers. The front brake will have a longer bolt. This is because the front bolt needs to go through the fork. There may be some curved washers on the front and rear brake that will sit flush around the fork crown and/or rear brake bridge. If you have a fork crown that's slightly curved, don't lose these! They are like hens' teeth and you will need them.
- Place the front brake through the fork, making sure any washers are flush against the crown, and the brake is centred. If you have curved washers, one will usually go at the front of the crown and one will go at the back.
- Tighten the nut with the appropriate tool.
- Do the same with the rear brake.

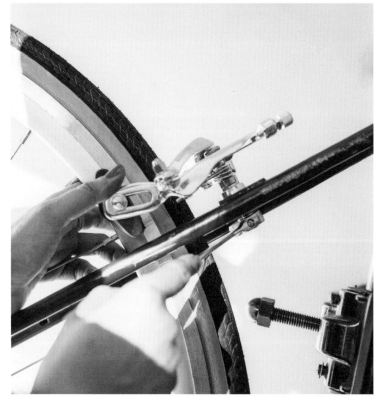

16

Attach the brake pads

Once the brakes are on, you can install and adjust the brake pads to the proper setting. Many road pads are sided, so if a pad says 'R' it will go on the right side of the bike, and 'L' will go on the left. Some even have a forward direction arrow.

- Start by putting the brake pad in the brake caliper. If there's a washer, it will be on the outside of the brake arm, underneath the bolt head.
- Hand-tighten the bolt, but don't use the hex key just yet.
- Once both pads are in, squeeze the brake caliper towards the rim with one hand. This way you can see where the pad hits the rim and line it up properly.
- Keep squeezing those arms! It's at this point where you'll make the final adjustment of the brake pad position. Make sure the pad isn't so high that it's touching the tyre, but also not so low that the bottom of the pad is coming off the braking surface of the wheel rim.
- Use a hex key to tighten the bolt; you'll want to make it fairly tight. Towards the end

the brake pad may twist in the direction you're turning. To avoid this, just make sure you hold the brake pad in the correct position before doing a final turn.

- Repeat this on the other side, and on the rear caliper as well.

17

Attach the brake levers

The position of brake levers will depend on the type of handlebars you have. You can always make minute adjustments when you've finished attaching the brake cable, but you need to get the levers as close as possible to the correct position.

Drop bar brake levers

• Slide on the brake levers, and align the end tip of the lever with the bottom edge of the handlebars. This is a good position to start with.
• Tighten the bolt. Make sure both of the levers are at the same height as well.

Cross-top/flat bar brake levers

• If you have flat bars, position the brake levers far enough apart so that the cables coming out of the levers won't interact with each other, but close enough that there's plenty room for your hands to rest fully on the bars. If the bars are narrow then the levers might end up being quite close.
• To make sure the brake cables don't butt up against each other, position one lever slightly lower than the other, or use bendable V-brake noodles as your ferrules (small metal sheaths that protect the end of the cable where it fits into components). If you have a swept-back type of handlebar, you have more leeway with positioning, but think ergonomically.

• Keep your hand's braking position in line with your arm. The angle of the levers should be where you're resting your hands on the bars – they are a continuation of the angle your arm and hands make. This angle can be adjusted later, once the cables have been installed.

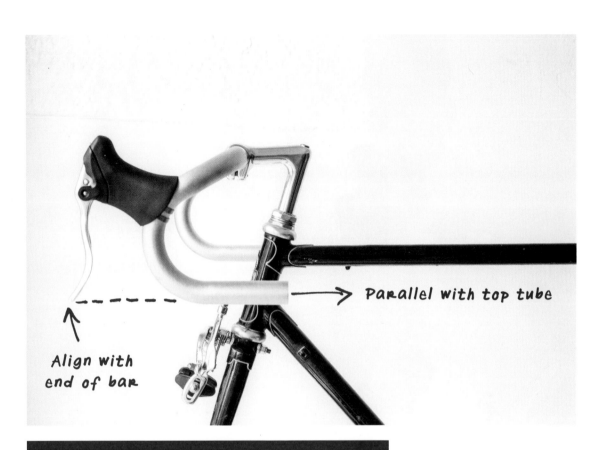

Parallel with top tube

Align with
end of bar

Which side of the handlebars should you put your front and rear brake levers on?

In countries where people drive on the left side of the road, it's customary to put your rear brake on the left side of your bike. This is so that when you're turning right, you're braking with your weaker brake while signalling with your right hand to cross traffic. Conversely, if you're riding in a country where people drive on the right side of the road, you'll put your rear brake on the right side of your bike. In the grand scheme of things it doesn't matter too much, as you should brake with two hands as much as possible anyway, but consider it a safety precaution. Braking with your more powerful brake one-handed can be a jarring experience!

Attach the brake cables and housing

- When cutting housing (the plastic outer covering) it's imperative you use enough to allow for ease of movement, both for the cable and for steering – but not so much that you create unnecessary twists and turns causing more friction between the cable and the housing. To that end, remember to measure twice.
- Front cable housing is easier to install than rear, as you don't need to take into consideration movement from steering. Take the brake housing and measure from the barrel adjuster or cup on the lever to the barrel adjuster on the front brake. If you have flat-bar levers or aero levers, there should be a gentle bend in the cable, about 90 degrees, no less. If you have old-fashioned road levers where the cable pops out of the top of the lever, make sure the curves are gentle, and that angles are around 90 degrees. Cut this length, and file the metal ends of the cable so the metal isn't sharp or pointing towards the centre of the cable.
- Use a tiny hex key or ballpoint pen to 'clear the airway' of the plastic inner

Turn 90 degrees

lining of the cable. Then, if your barrel adjusters allow for ferrules, add a ferrule to each end of the cable.

• Rear cable housing is a bit trickier. If your frame has braze-on cable stops (ie they're a permanent fixture on the frame) on the top tube, use these to hold the pieces of cable housing. If you have the kind of cable stops that aren't closed at one end (like they're just a tube), that means you'll need to use a full length of housing across the top tube. And if you don't have cable stops at all, you'll need to use cable ties, or housing clamps, to hold the entire length of cable housing across the top tube.

• For those of you with cable stops that are closed at one end, cut your front piece of brake housing by holding one end at the brake lever barrel adjuster, and the other end at the first braze-on. Turn your handlebars so that they are 90 degrees away from the centre line. Make sure that the cable housing is long enough so that it's just barely touching your head tube, note the length, and cut here. If the housing hits the frame before you can make a full turn, it could pull the brake cable while you are turning!

• With the back piece, hold one end of the brake housing at the cable stop, and the other end at the barrel adjuster on the rear brake. It needs to be long enough to reach and fit comfortably, but not so long it is bending up.

• Note the length and cut here. File down the metal ends and place a ferrule on each end, if your frame and/ or brakes allow for one.

• If you don't have cable stops, you'll need to cut brake housing the full length of your bike. Start by placing one end of the housing at the front brake barrel adjuster. Next, bring the housing all the way to the rear brake barrel adjuster. Turn the handlebars 90 degrees to make sure that when you turn, the housing isn't touching the frame. Also, hold the cable against the top tube while measuring. Cut this length, and file down the metal ends. Open the plastic lining at each end, then place a ferrule on each end.

Perfect length

- Get the correct brake cable for your type of brakes (see p103). Insert the cable so that the cable end fully sits in its cup or cage. Thread the cable through the brake housing and through the anchor bolt, or clamp on the brake caliper.
- With one hand, hold the brake arms down so the pads are against the rim, and with your other hand, pull the cable taut. Use a hex key or spanner to tighten the bolt that will hold the cable in place. Tighten.
- If the cable is new you need to 'bed in' the cable, ferrules and housing. Over time, the housing will compress, causing the cable to become looser. By pre-compressing it, it won't squish as much over time, reducing the problem of sluggish braking. Once the cable has been fixed into place, squeeze the brake lever hard five times. You'll see the brake cable become slack, possibly to the point where you'll need to undo the cable bolt, pull off the slack, and retighten the bolt. Or it may slacken just enough so that the pads come off the rim. Either way, you want to make sure the brake pads aren't touching the rim when you spin the wheel, and the

brake is responsive when you pull the lever. How responsive is up to you; I prefer my brakes to be pretty sharp. Use this opportunity to double check the brake pads aren't touching the tyre or coming off the bottom of the rim, and adjust if necessary.
- With cable cutters, cut the cables leaving 4-5cm spare, then using pliers, 'crimp' an end cap on to secure. I use the cutting edge of pliers to make indentations in the cap.

Centring the brake

- If you have dual pivot calipers, they will probably have a grub screw that will allow you to centre the brake calipers.
- If one of the brake arms is hitting the rim before the other one, adjusting the grub screw will move the calipers side to side, allowing you to centre the caliper with respect to the wheel. Just be sure to watch the caliper carefully when you adjust!

A word about internal cable routing

- If you have a frame that has two holes in the top tube, one at the front and one at the back, you have internal cable routing, designed for the rear brake cable to run through. A posh bike will have an inner guide for cable, but a cheaper frame will not – and this is where you'll run into problems.
- To test this, put a cable through the front hole and see if it pops up out of the back hole. If it does, you've got some gorgeous internal routing going on. But if it doesn't, and you're poking around like you're searching for a light switch in a dark room, don't despair.
- If your frame is not steel, you can use a magnet to guide a galvanised steel cable towards the back hole.
- If it is steel, try the old thread and vacuum technique. Tie a piece of thread to the end of the cable. Put the thread in one end of the frame, and put a vacuum to the other end. The suction should pull the thread out the other side, and you should be able to gently pull the cable through.
- If all else fails, Jagwire makes an internal cable routing tool, or you can ignore it and run the cable housing outside across the whole top tube – cable ties are so useful.
- In future, make sure either the cable or cable housing is always inside the frame – that way you'll have a placeholder. I have to admit, internal routing is swish and *can* be worth it.

How to use barrel adjusters

• The cups that brake cable housing sit in are very important. Barrel adjusters can screw in and out of the brake lever or brake caliper, and are a way of tightening and loosening brake cables without using tools.

• When you first install brake cables, make sure the barrel adjusters are screwed all the way in.

• Over time, when the brake cable housing compresses and the pads start to wear down, you can unscrew the barrel adjusters to tighten the cable. They work like this: although the cable is being held between two fixed points, the barrel adjuster is changing the length of the cable housing, which tightens and loosens the cable depending on which direction the adjuster is being turned.

19

Fit the seatpost and saddle

• If you have an old-fashioned seatpost, the kind that is just a tube, attach the clamp to the seatpost. (Maybe even attach your saddle to the clamp first.) This will prevent the seatpost from dropping into the depths of the bike!

• Put copper paste or grease on the inside of the seat tube. Glide the seatpost in, ensuring the minimum insertion point is not visible.

• With the bike on the ground, adjust the saddle height. A good starting position is with the saddle a few centimetres below your hip. If you're using your bike for commuting, you want to be able to easily put your foot down when you stop. If you're riding long distances, this isn't as important, and you could position the saddle at hip height. Point the saddle forward and tighten the seat bolt. Make sure that the saddle is parallel with the ground and adjust the seat clamp if necessary. Again, adjustments are just that – you can change the forward/back/up/down positions to suit your bum's tastes.

20

Attach the grips

• Some grips bolt on – a grub screw holds it in place after you slide it on.

• A hot tip for slide-on grips – use rubbing alcohol or hairspray! Spray a bit inside the grip, then slide it on to the handlebar. It'll go on real easy.

• See p152 for how to wrap bar tape instead of grips.

ACCESSORIES

Accessories are the icing on the cake of a bike. They'll provide some more personality for your build, and while it's a very subjective choice, nothing is permanent. You can also add things that will change how you use your bicycle - a rack or basket will make it more commuter friendly, while dynamo lights will ensure you never have to worry about batteries ever again. And don't forget to get a lock!

BRIGHT THINKING: LIGHTS

Lights are required by law in many countries, and are just plain common sense. Flashing lights are great for getting attention, but they don't help drivers gauge distance, so some sort of combination of a flashing light plus a solid beam is a good combo. Also consider other cyclists and pedestrians' eyesight when choosing lights. You might think super-bright lights are the best to alert drivers, but they can be aggressive and inconsiderate towards fellow road users.

Look into lights that are coloured with a tint of blue (blue travels farthest in the colour spectrum), lights that are visible from the side as well as the front, or ones that are just plain bonkers. I use a set of VeloHalo wheel lights that weave through the spokes, and I get compliments on them all the time, even from cab drivers.

If you're out on lost lanes, or a secret forest path, it's way more important to have lights that will help you see where you're going. To light a road path, you'll want lights that are at least 300 lumens, and if you're in the uncharted wilderness, get something over 1000 lumens.

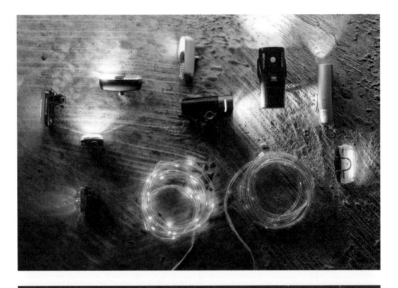

All about dynamos

Dynamos are awesome. You never have to worry about dead batteries or recharging your lights, and LED technology has made the lights mega-bright. They are available in a range of budgets.

Dynamos are a blanket term for a type of generator that converts the movement of the bike into an electrical current that turns on lights. There are generally two options here: tyre (aka 'bottle' dynamos – guess what their shape looks like), and hub dynamos. Both use the motion of the bicycle to send a charge to a light, or in the case of some fancier contraptions that have come out, to a battery that holds the charge.

There are also dynamos that use magnets, one on a stationary point on a frame, the other on a spoke, and every time they pass they create a charge. It's like a friction-free generator that harnesses the power of magnetic fields.

MAKE YOURSELF HEARD:
BELLS AND HORNS

If you're a city cyclist, chances are you are going to need to amplify your presence amongst the Muggles (read: people who don't ride bikes). This is for both your safety and theirs. Bells are a polite way to do this, but for those who take on heavy traffic, air horns can alert cars to your presence in the most audible way possible. Bells are also a really lovely way to accessorise your bike. My personal fave is the big ding-dong bell. Its sound is loud, authoritarian and pleasing, and I can't help but smile every time I ring it.

THE BIKE'S HAIRSTYLE: BAR TAPE AND GRIPS

I absolutely insist you get some form of bar tape or grips. They make your bike really comfortable to ride, protect your hands and add a nifty look. Also, the ends of your handlebars must be covered or plugged, to prevent something called 'coring' – as in apple coring. There are horror stories about people who get into crashes and their handlebars go through their legs (and other body parts) because the ends weren't protected. Most bar tape comes with plugs, but if not, you can use a wine bottle cork. At a pinch.

How to wrap bar tape for drop-bars

Good-looking bar tape is a beautiful thing, but wrapping it seems to be a love-or-hate thing for people. I personally love it, and I take great care in making sure that my spacing and tension are even.

There are *so* many different types of bar tape out there that choosing one can feel paralysing, but luckily bar tape is changeable, so if you get tired of your current style or colour or handfeel (that's not a real word – yet), it's easy to change to another one.

There are many ways of wrapping bar tape, so if this method doesn't work for you, or you'd like to find other ways, as ever, the internet is your friend.

• To start, you'll need to make sure that your brakes are in the position that you want them to be in. There's room for small adjustments, but not loads, so take the bike for a spin and make sure you like where they're placed.

• If you have aero brake levers where the cables come out the back towards the handlebars, now's the time to tape the cable housing against the handlebars. Depending on where the housing exits the lever, you'll either want to place the housing at the front of the bar or at the back. Don't put it on the top, as this will be uncomfortable for your hands. Some modern handlebars have a groove to accommodate the housing here – use it! It will create a nice round handfeel. Use electrical

tape to attach the housing to the bars. Make sure you allow enough housing so that you can swivel your bars comfortably to the right and left, and the housing doesn't tighten up against the frame when you turn the bars.

• If you have old-fashioned drop brakes where the cables pop out of the levers on the top, there's no need to tape the cables down.

• On both sides of the handlebars you'll be starting at the bottom end of the bars, wrapping the tape in a circular motion from the inside of the bike, up, over, and away from your bike.

• Pull back the hoods of the brake lever.

• Unroll one of the tapes and peel off a couple of inches of the sticky backing paper. Place the edge of the tape at the bottom opening of the bars, perpendicular from the bar, with the roll of tape on the inside of the bike.

• Line up the edge of the sticky bit with the edge of the handlebar and press on.

• Bring the tape up and over, away from the bicycle and then back down, completing the first circle around your bar. Pull taut but not tight! You don't want to overstretch the tape and potentially snap it.

- At this point, bring the tape back up and away from the bike, but angle it about 30 degrees from the edge of the handlebar.

- Bring the tape around the bottom, back towards the bicycle and up again. When you do this, line up the edge of the sticky bit with the edge of the bartape as you go around, making sure the sticky bit is touching the bar and not the tape – this will make sure that you keep an even spacing and prevent it from slipping around when you ride. Remember to pull taut.

- When you approach the lever you have two options. One is to use the extra rectangular square that probably came with the box of tape. If it didn't, cut your own 7-8cm piece. Peel off the backing paper and wrap around the unsightly band holding the brake lever in place.

- Your other option is to use the 'figure of eight' method, which doesn't use this extra rectangle.

Figure-of-eight method

- Upon approaching your lever, make sure the tape is completely wrapped along the bottom of the lever. Then, bringing the tape from the inside to the outside, pull the tape diagonally up across the unsightly metal band, and over the top and back down.

- Continue the '8' by bringing the tape over the unsightly metal band and then pull the tape to the front of the bike and underneath the brake, diagonally up and back around the handlebars. At this point, the unsightly metal band should be mostly covered up with an X shape.

- Bring the tape up and over the top of the brake lever now, and then continue to wrap your tape around as you were before, pulling taut.

Ending

- Stop 4cm or so between the bar tape and stem, before the point where many bars get wider. To finish, you want to keep the nice diagonal angle going, but finish the tape parallel with the stem. To do this, you'll need to cut your bar tape at an angle.

- Pull the tape away from the bar, keeping the diagonal going. Place scissors parallel with the stem and cut the bar tape parallel with the stem, still holding the diagonal alignment. You should have a severe diagonal cut on your tape; as you wrap this around the handlebar, it will create an edge parallel with the stem.

- Use insulating tape to finish, pop down the hoods, and don't forget the bar-end plugs. If they're slightly too small, wrap insulating tape round the insertion side a couple of times.

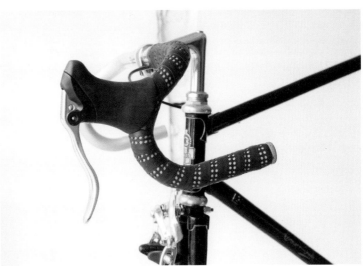

CARRY MORE: RACKS AND BASKETS

Racks and baskets are great ways to portage your bits about. Get it off your back and on to your bike! If your bike has eyelets on the fork, seat stays and/or dropouts then you're ready to pack it in.

Pannier racks are an easy attachment that will allow you to carry panniers and other rack-friendly bags (imagine your bike as a mule). You can get racks for both the front and rear of the bike. If you're a heavy person, try getting a front pannier rack to help distribute weight evenly across the bike. Many frames won't have eyelets on the seat stays, but you can always use P-clips to help attach a rear rack to the frame. And make sure you get a rack that's correctly sized for your wheels.

Baskets are even more convenient. They're easily accessible for your hands when they're up front, and when they're in the back on top of your pannier rack they help carry even more stuff. Some even detach and let you carry your kit. If you have drop bars, you're not going to be able to fit a conventional basket, but there are handlebar bags that can provide a similar set-up, which is great for touring. Flat bars aren't ideal for baskets as your hand placement and brake cables can get awkward, so if you're really after a front basket, swept-back bars are the best match. An option for flat bars is to get a front flat rack. This will sit below the bars and still allow you to carry stuff on top (like pizza!) while keeping your hands and cables free from interaction.

PROTECT YOURSELF: MUDGUARDS

Mudguards protect your backside and your bike from rain and mud, but they're an important part of social dynamics as well. All that spray from your back tyre can go straight out behind you and into a fellow rider's face. Best to get your butt covered.

You need to make sure that you've got enough clearance for a mudguard first. This is the gap between your tyre and your brake. If you've got at least 2cm, then you should be OK.

There are different types of mudguards: full, clip-on, and partial mudguards are the major categories. First you need to check for eyelets. These will be on your fork ends and rear dropouts. If you don't have eyelets, that's fine too, but you'll have to get clip-on mudguards instead. The other thing you need to know is what size of tyre you have – this will help you choose the right size of mudguard.

Full mudguards
Full mudguards give you complete coverage, preventing spray from soaking you, your bike and other road users. You can get full mudguards to fit almost every size of tyre – but be sure you get the right size! The wrong size could mean the tyre ends up rubbing against the guard, or not fitting in between the brake and the tyre.

Clip-on mudguards
These are quick-fitting mudguards that are usually strapped on to the seat stays and forks. They are great for racing bikes that don't have eyelets. The company SKS makes long clip-on mudguards to make sure that you're fully covered.

Partial
Great for emergencies, partial mudguards can sort you out in

a tight spot. Ass Savers mudguards pop in under the saddle, but don't take care of social spray (as in, the person cycling behind you will still get your tyre spray). There are also partial guards designed for mountain bikes (but will work just fine for road bikes), like the SKS X-Tra Dry guards that fit on your seatpost. I call it a beavertail. In a tight spot, you can always stash a plastic litre bottle in the little triangle above your rear brake bridge and seat stays.

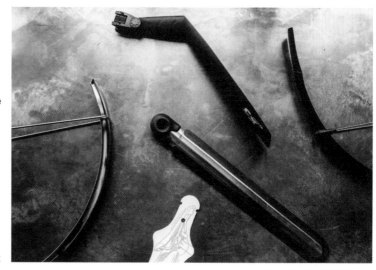

STAY HYDRATED: BOTTLE CAGES

If you're touring or on long rides, you want to carry water on your bike, not on your back. In order to fit a conventional bottle cage, you need bottle cage bosses. These are rivet-nuts on the down tube and/or seat tube. You can simply screw in your bottle cage on here.

But what if you don't have bosses? Don't dehydrate – there are loads of alternatives. Handlebar bottle cages attach to bars, but beware that the weight of your filled bottle could cause it to swivel downwards (voice of experience here). There are time

trial bottle cages that attach to the back of the saddle. And people are finally coming out with alternatives to traditional cages that strap to the bike frame. Check out King Cage and Monkii Cage for some inventive ways to carry water bottles.

KEEP YOUR BIKE YOURS: LOCKS AND CHAINS

If you've spent this much time and energy on creating your beautiful beast, you best get some form of security for your bike pronto, especially if you live in a city notorious for bicycle theft. There are a couple of ways of judging how much to spend. The first is the old classic of 'spend 10% of what your bike is worth' on a lock. This method works for new bikes, but for secondhand bikes, family heirlooms or ones that have seen some restoration work, this isn't going to cut it.

Another way of figuring out how much to spend on security is, 'How much would you spend to get your bike back if it was stolen?' Some bikes are even considered priceless, in which case they should only ever be in one of three places: at home safely indoors, in your sightline at all times, or under your butt.

D-locks and chain locks are the classics. Get one that is sold secure rated, either bronze, silver, or gold. Note that most bike insurance companies will require you to have a gold-rated lock. Abus and Kryptonite are highly rated, and Kryptonite even offers an opt-

in anti-theft protection guarantee.

Cables and cable locks aren't as hench as your sold secure D-locks, but they're still a deterrent. They make good secondary locks that can go through saddles and wheels. On the plus side they're lightweight and easy to carry around, but on the other hand they're fairly easy to cut through with bolt cutters. Trust me, I've seen it done. It's not pretty.

Security skewers and bolts are a great way to ensure your quick-release wheels, seatpost bolt, saddle bolts and stem bolts stay right where they are. Many use a special key, so you have to keep this on you at all times, but consider it another version of a lock, and a lightweight one at that. Those five-sided skewers are also OK, but the matching keys are fairly easy to get online, and I've even managed to take them off with mole grips. A new entry to the market is the HexLox security magnet, which fits into any common six-sided allen bolt.

BASIC MAINTENANCE

There's a difference between maintenance and repair. You know the saying, an ounce of prevention is worth a pound of cure? Well, maintenance is prevention and repair is that costly cure. The little things you do in the here and now will prevent full-blown catastrophes that blow your budget and your bike. Take the time to do these simple actions. You've spent so much time creating your gorgeous ride - don't leave it to fend for itself in the big bad world. Remember, basic maintenance will ensure that your bike is happy and treats you well.

So, how often will you need to perform maintenance? This is a question I get asked a lot – and the answer is always 'It depends.' The more you ride, the more you're going to have to do it. (Another excuse to have multiple bikes, eh?) I've put in a general answer to this question in each of the following sections.

Regardless, pay attention to your bike – a quiet bike is a happy bike, and if it's making sounds, it's your bike speaking to you. Listen to what it's saying. Squeaks often mean metal is rubbing on metal, and it could be simply something needing a bit of oil. Rattling means something is loose that shouldn't be, so you'll need to tighten something.

Here are the sort of basic things you'll need to get:

- Old T-shirts
- Old toothbrushes
- Bucket
- Bike-specific cleaner
- Chain-specific cleaner or rubbing alcohol
- Chain oil

CHAIN UPKEEP

Cleaning the chain

The chain is the canary in the coalmine of the drivetrain. Once that goes, it's a sign the rest of the drivetrain is on its way out. Ignore at your peril. Clean your chain with the seasons, and it (and the other components) will last longer. Generally speaking, if you ride to work every day in the city, change your chain once a year.

• Use a rubber band to stick two toothbrushes together so the brush heads are facing each other. Follow the directions on the bottle of chain-specific cleaner, as they are not all the same. You can also use rubbing alcohol. It's a cheap and environmentally friendly cleaner that can be used on bike parts.

• Spray your choice of cleaner on the chain, and use the two brush heads to scrub the top and bottom of the chain. This is more important than cleaning the sides.

• Rinse off with water and dry with a clean rag.

• Another option is to soak the chain in cola overnight. You'll end up with a sparkling clean chain. (Makes you think about that fizzy pop you're drinking, doesn't it?)

Oiling the chain

• Start on the bottom part of the chain, on the inside. Put one drop of oil on each bushing, rotating the cranks slowly backwards. Don't drizzle oil on top of your freewheel, it's just going to gunk up everything on the hub.

• Let it sink in for five to ten minutes, whizz the chain around several times to distribute more of the oil, then – this is the important part – *wipe off as much as you humanly can*. Excess oil attracts dirt and grit, and the paste it forms wears down a drivetrain faster.

CLEANING THE RIMS

This one simple trick will help your wheels last longer and brake more efficiently. When you brake, those bits of dirt and dust scour the rims like sandpaper, scraping the walls down faster than is necessary. All you need is a clean damp cloth of some sort to wipe down the rims. Do this every couple of weeks or so, and do it more often in inclement weather, especially if roads have been gritted with salt. Salt will wear down your components faster.

CHANGING THE BRAKE PADS

While you're down there wiping your rims, check your pads for wear. New brake pads have grooves, and some even have a wear line. If these grooves are gone and the pad is flat or has reached the wear line, you must change these pads straight away. Pads often have a metal post inside, and you could be dangerously close to exposing this. And guess what braking with metal will do to your rims?

Sometimes brake pads are 'sided', meaning one will be made for the left side of the bike, and one will be made for the right. They will usually be labelled if so. Some also say 'forward' which means that it will need to point in the forward direction of the bike. When you put your pads on, make sure they are not touching the tyre, nor are they coming off the bottom of the flat part of the rim. Unevenly placed pads will cause uneven wear and inefficient braking (and possibly an exploding tyre).

Get thee to a bike shop and change those pads!

CHANGING THE BRAKE CABLES

Brake cables wear over time. They may fray, and at this point they could even snap. If your bike is outside a lot, water can sneak inside the housing and cause rust and aluminium corrosion. Changing them every so often, depending on how much you ride (and how much you brake!), will result in a noticeable increase in braking performance for safer stopping. It's easy to do this – just follow the instructions of how to remove the brake cables (p50) then how to fit them (p142). If you see any rust or tears on the housing, be sure to replace this as well.

KEEP THE TYRES PUMPED

There's an enthralling CyclingTips podcast featuring the wonderful Jan Heine, where he argues that wide tyres with very low pressure are actually more efficient than skinny, hard tyres in the racing world. You should check it out if you're obsessed like me.

But, conventionally speaking, when you're riding through the city on poor-quality roads, tyres pumped up to their correct pressure will help prevent punctures. Invest in a good-quality track pump with a gauge, and pump up your tyres every couple of weeks. Otherwise, any local bicycle shop worth its salt will have a track pump outside you can use. Add some Panaracer Flataway Kevlar tape to the inside of your tyre for extra protection, and avoid pothole like the plague!

PS: If you want to learn more about bicycles and maintenance, your next port of call should be Shelley Lynn Jackson and Ethan Clark's Chainbreaker Bike Book, and the Sheldon Brown website. And if you like retro guides, check out Richard Ballantine's bicycle books.

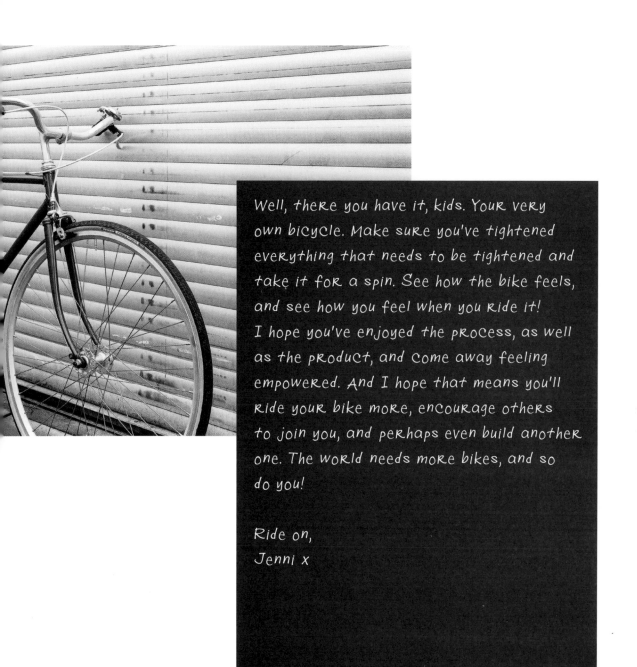

Well, there you have it, kids. Your very own bicycle. Make sure you've tightened everything that needs to be tightened and take it for a spin. See how the bike feels, and see how you feel when you ride it! I hope you've enjoyed the process, as well as the product, and come away feeling empowered. And I hope that means you'll ride your bike more, encourage others to join you, and perhaps even build another one. The world needs more bikes, and so do you!

Ride on,
Jenni x

INDEX

INDEX

INDEX

ACKNOWLEDGEMENTS

This book is dedicated to my dad, George, who taught me how to use a soldering iron when I was eight years old. Thanks, daddy – you were the one who planted the seed for me to become a mechanic, and also told me I could be anything I wanted to be. The world needs more kind and encouraging people like you.

Ichiban numero uno thanks to Euan Ferguson, London Bike Kitchen member 692, who helped publicise LBK and then put my publisher, Frances Lincoln, in touch with me. Without your kind but firm prodding, I don't think I would've gotten as far as I did.

Inspirational thanks to my commissioning editor Zena Alkayat – your immense professionalism and kindness were the essential foundation to get me going.

'We're not worthy' thanks to Glenn Howard, designer extraordinaire – your Tetris powers to move everything around and make it look amazing are mindblowing.

'How does she do it' thanks to Erika Raxworthy – your wizardry managed to make our boring tools look like they have magical powers.

Of course I have to thank my mom, Miho – your unwavering support and unconditional love have been a rock for me.

Thank you to my sister Candice, who has written countless books already, and whose work ethic continues to be an inspiration.

Glamorous thanks to my part-time hand models: Jools Walker, Naomi Mahendran and Christopher Nelson. Thank you for lending a hand. Ha!

Ultra-mega thank yous to the local shops and businesses that sorted out my frantic searches for specific bike bits: SBC Cycles, The Hackney Peddler, Isambard's, Auguste Handmade, Freshtripe, Silverfish, ZyroFisher, Blaze, Michaux Club, Cole Coatings, Pelago, Brick Lane Bikes, Look Mum No Hands.

Nerdy technical editing thanks to: Megan Somerville and Elle Smith. Thank you so much for going through my text with a fine-tooth comb and a mechanical mindset.

Seb Achaibou, Monika Zamojska, Laurie Garnons-Williams, Jools Walker, Pi Manson, Josh Lane, Shibb Bromwich – thank you for reading previous drafts and for your feedback.

Hackney Libraries and Ziferblat – thank you for being my book-writing caves.

Thank you to my old boss, Hannah Kowszun - you showed me the power of word-smithing and made me a better writer.

Bear hugs to my bike gang here in London, for all your support and encouragement: Caren, Seb, Alex, Naomi, Jools, Jacqui, Mon, Ester, Juliet, Laurie, Nelsy, Tim.

And a final massive thank you to all the LBK members and friends who have been so wonderful! This book is for all of you.

How to Build a Bike

© 2017 Quarto Publishing plc

Text © Jenni Gwiazdowski 2017
Photographs © Erika Raxworthy 2017
Commissioning editor: Zena Alkayat
Edited by Euan Ferguson
Designed by Glenn Howard

First Published in 2017 by Frances Lincoln,
an imprint of The Quarto Group.
The Old Brewery, 6 Blundell Street,
London N7 9BH, United Kingdom.
T (0)20 7700 6700 F (0)20 7700 8066
www.QuartoKnows.com

A catalogue record for this book is available from the British Library.

ISBN 978 0 7112 3898 5

Printed and bound in China

5 6 7 8 9